Francis Stanley

St. Petersburg to Plevna

Containing interviews with leading Russian statesmen and generals

Francis Stanley

St. Petersburg to Plevna
Containing interviews with leading Russian statesmen and generals

ISBN/EAN: 9783337165062

Printed in Europe, USA, Canada, Australia, Japan

Cover: Foto ©ninafisch / pixelio.de

More available books at **www.hansebooks.com**

ST. PETERSBURG TO PLEVNA.

CONTAINING

Interviews with leading Russian Statesmen and Generals.

BY

FRANCIS STANLEY,

SPECIAL WAR CORRESPONDENT OF THE "GOLOSS" OF RUSSIA,
"MANCHESTER GUARDIAN," ETC.

LONDON:

RICHARD BENTLEY AND SON,

NEW BURLINGTON STREET.

1878.

CONTENTS.

CHAPTER VII.

CHAPTER VIII.

CHAPTER IX.

CHAPTER X.

FROM ST. PETERSBURG TO PLEVNA.

CHAPTER I.

ACTING on the instructions of a leading provincial
paper, which I had undertaken to represent at the
seat of war, I left England on the 16th of May for
St. Petersburg, well provided, by private influential
friends at home, with letters to the leading politicians
and ministers of Russia, who had not at that epoch
left for Bucharest, or the seat of war on the Danube.

It is not my intention, in the few chapters I am
now offering to the public, to deal with anything
which has not a direct bearing on the great questions
of the hour, leaving to a future opportunity the story
of my experiences or adventures, so far as they are

1

purely of a personal character.   I propose to confine myself to the relation of the confidences extended to me by the leading men I have met, and to the action of the different armies, corps d'armées, and divisions with which I have been brought in contact during six months' stay at the front.

In conformity with a rule I have laid down never to knock at great men's doors, or rather at the doors of men in great places, without being first assured of a good reception, I wrote, on my arrival in St. Petersburg, to Count Schouvaloff, asking the honour of an interview, and mentioning by whom I had been furnished with a letter of introduction.   The course of the following day brought an answer, requesting me to call on him at his house on the 23rd of May.   Going there on that date, the "Suisse" informed me that his Excellency was out.   I opened my pocket-book, replaced it in my pocket lighter by ten roubles, and the "Suisse," without even an apologetic change of a single muscle of his face, informed me that his Excellency had left word I was to be shown up.   This Russian system of exacting "backsheesh," to a greater extent than even that of Turkey, pervades all the serving classes in Russia.

The Count Schouvaloff, dressed in the uniform of

an Aide-de-camp General of the Empire, received me with a civil shake of the hand, and seating me opposite him, at a small writing-table, asked me at once, in the true style of an ancient grand maître de la police,* why I had come to the capital, what I wanted, the name of the paper I represented, and invited me to lead the conversation by asking what particular point I wished to be advised on.

I put it to him shortly—first, why he was in St. Petersburg, and not, at so critical a moment, at his post in London? Secondly, what guarantee Russia could offer to prove that her object, in attacking Turkey, was in reality the welfare of the Christian races, not the projects of aggrandisement for which the world in general, and England in particular, gave her credit?

" I am not in England at the present moment," his Excellency replied, " first, on account of the very discourteous tone of the late despatch, written May 6, by your Minister for Foreign Affairs, Lord Derby, to our Foreign Office; the substance of which is not so displeasing to us in the matter contained, as in the

---

* N.B.—Count Schouvaloff was grand maître de la police et chef de gendarmerie before being appointed Ambassador to England.

manner in which it is submitted. That despatch has
rendered personal intercourse with him and others,
whom I regard as warm friends, almost impossible
for the moment; since Russia, and I as her representative, cannot but feel hurt at England's assuming
towards us the same dictatorial tone in this delicate
Eastern question, as she usually assumes to a recal-
citrant colony, an independent Dutch state, or the
Swiss Confederation, when making some demand of
extradition, or excusing the shelter afforded to a
refugee. In answer to your other question, neither
my Emperor nor the country (*même le pays*) pretend
to disguise, even for a moment, the vital interests
both have in the neutrality of England in this war
(if her approbation cannot be obtained) being strictly
maintained. Both are desirous of giving every
assurance, public and private, that this war is a
consequence of the unanimous wish of the people of
the Russian dominions to come to the aid of their
co-religionists, and the personal desire of the Emperor is to be the avenging instrument of Europe on
Turkish misrule. The prejudices existing in the
minds of a large portion of the English people
are unworthy, and the fears of alarmists are un-
warranted. What," continued he, "has England

to fear from Russia ? Has not calmness always succeeded the frantic popular outbursts of this Eastern
craze (*maladie*) ? Did not England, half a century
ago, fear for India, because we were coquetting with
the Caucasian seaboard ? Was not India, according
to your Russophobes, menaced because we had seized
Khiva, and so on ? And now the cry is, that Constantinople, the taking of which you suppose to mean
the injury of British interests, is in danger. Let
those who cry look to the natural defences of that
city ; consider, but for a moment, in order to dissi-
pate their foolish fright, its position on the map
relative to the present distribution of European
power, and the fact that the Black Sea is in
reality a Turkish lake. Though controlled by none,
yet our treaties with our friendly neighbour,
Germany, would, even were we in line before
Adrianople, prevent our usurping the gates of the
Bosphorus, or abolishing the freedom of the
Danube. That we shall require, in proportion to
the sacrifices we are compelled to make, certain
advantages, I cannot undertake to deny ; but they
cannot be of a nature to cause anxiety to England,
or alarm to her ally, Austria. Russia is combating
on account of the sympathetic feeling existing between

races of the same religion ; and not for the change
to a more genial clime of a population tired of colds
and snow, as is generally imputed to her.   In one
word," said the Count Schouvaloff, " if England cannot, or will not, give us credence for good faith, let
her at least not doubt our sanity by supposing we
can ignore that a march on Constantinople (be we
successful in crossing the Balkans) would mean
Europe in arms against us."

The day following my interview with the Count
Schouvaloff, I presented letters of introduction to
the Count Greig, Admiral in the Russian Navy and
Comptroller-General of the Empire.   At that interview, and in many a subsequent one, I could not
but feel struck with the lucidity of the explanations
he offered me on Russia's foreign policy and her
internal government, conversing all the time in pure
English, never at a loss for a word, and apparently
thoroughly satisfied that the form of government of
which he was a member and a champion, was the
only one adapted to the welfare of the Russian
nation.   His subtle comparison of the Russian
Council of Ministers with our own House of Parliament, his explanation of the practical working of
the Senate, and his suggestion, as he talked, that

there was, as in England, an actual organised opposition to the too great increase of ministerial
power, charmed me, but failed to convince.

"The ministers are responsible," said he, "individually to the Great Council of State, collectively
to the Emperor. Therefore, as you will perceive,
they are checked in carrying any measure, however
individually they may desire its success, by the fact
that it must have the support of the majority of the
Council of State, before whom it is laid for sanction,
before it becomes law. A vote is taken, as in
your Houses of Parliament, and the ayes or the
noes have it, as with you."

"Yes," said I, "but what have the people to say
in the appointment of the Council of the Senate?
Are not its members taken from the high functionary
class, and from those of the class in favour with the
Emperor? and cannot each one be made and un-
made at his will?"

"Of course," replied the Count; "but the sons of
the people can, by energy, and luck, and education,
attain to the class from which these men are chosen.
What more can they possibly want? Has not the
people itself its own representation, its local government, its internal and separate administration of

justice? Russia is divided into sixty governments, with a governor appointed by the Emperor, but with courts and local administration entirely independent of Imperial pressure. Commencing with the peasants, the smaller cases requiring the interference of justice are left entirely in their own hands; brawls, quarrels over property, theft, are decided by three of the oldest inhabitants of a village, elected by the suffrage of all the villagers. Again, the villagers of a district send a representative to a representative body formed in the largest town or seat of government of the district, where all local matters—as to roads and other public wants—are discussed and settled, without any interference on the part of the governor, who alone represents Imperial interests."

"But," ventured I, "when a tax is imposed by Imperial edict, and for Imperial interests, on a district, can the representatives of the towns and villages discuss and reject such an imposition?"

"No, of course not," returned his Excellency; "they can only register it, as, otherwise, each district would consider that it was the neighbouring one's duty to minister to Imperial wants. But they are at liberty to tax themselves as much as they please towards the making of roads, and towards other matters of general improvement."

" And do they do it ?"

" Well, no.—Our judges are, as you know, irremovable, and entirely independent of Imperial control; in fact, far too much so, as the Minister of Justice has not even as much control over them and their decisions as is desirable and necessary by reason of the great quantities of written laws in the statute-book of Russia—laws uncontrolled by registered precedents, and open to the interpretations laid down by the diverse minds of each separate judge. Then, again, our press, which that of other nations insists is gagged, is in reality not so. It is true that the censorship exists. But why ? Merely in the interest of the papers themselves (who, unfortunately, do not see it), and as a guide and check on public opinion in Russia, which, being now only in its infancy, would not be strong enough to support and judge the daily emanations likely to proceed from a young press, were it left entirely free to give utterance to all it would like to say or to sell. In fact," said the Admiral, " to sum up, our government is one of the freest and least despotic of all the governments of Europe. In no country do the people enjoy such complete liberty of action, and the *secousse* that is occasionally felt through society in Russia is solely attributable to the unwarrantable desire on the part of certain sections of that society to increase the liberties now accorded until they degenerate into license. The Government, hoping that such elements will dissolve of themselves, allow them to continue as long as possible, until at last it is compelled to put out its hand; and the sudden check of this seditious action, which, while looking arbitrary, is in reality lenient, gives opportunity to the enemies of Russia to point out the autocratic nature of a government that is in reality exceedingly democratic."

He was of course alluding to the state trials then about to take place at St. Petersburg.

Conversing another day with the Admiral on the foreign policy of the Government, and the terms of peace likely to be made when Russia should have fulfilled her mission across the Danube, he insisted that territorial aggrandisement was not Russia's object; that should she be successful her demands would be limited to Russia as it was in 1856, with the northern issue of the Danube; that considering the mid-channel to be an international work, Russia would in nowise attempt to interfere with it. The acquisition of Constantinople was not one, nor the opening of the Straits another, of the objects for which Russia had gone to war; though of course no distinct pledge could be given that the capital of the Turkish Empire would be held sacred, for in every war the enemy's capital was the legitimate object of military operations, yet the permanent occupation of Constantinople was not one of the objects for which Russia would have gone to war.

The declaration made by the Emperor at Livadia might be implicitly relied on. It was an error to say that the war in Russia was not popular, or that the Emperor himself had been hurried into it by the effects of a few incautious words uttered at Moscow. Russian politics were not so haphazard. General Ignatieff had on several occasions, when at Constantinople, informed the Porte that the rejection of the conditions of the Conference would be the signal for the uprising of the peoples of Russia to war; that the angry feeling in the country with respect to the Turkish oppression of the Christian subjects of Turkey had become so pronounced, that all classes were calling for the

Government to draw the sword to avenge and protect their co-religionists of Bulgaria.

The army itself, drawn as it was from the agricultural working-class, was 'eager to march and confident of victory. He himself, as Comptroller-General of the Empire, could assure me that no financial crisis need be expected to paralyse the efforts Russia was about to make.

Reviewing the Eastern question, he was of opinion that Turkey, as then existing, was in an anomalous position in regard to the rest of Europe, and could not be allowed to continue in that position.

The independence of Roumania, the separation of Bulgaria, the autonomy of Servia, Bosnia, and the Herzegovina, were imperatively called for. The Black Sea as a Turkish lake was quite as injurious to the interests of Russia, as the Black Sea turned into a Russian lake could be to Europe; successes in Armenia were no source of menace to England in India; the great cause of agitation in England over Russian conquests in Asia was the general ignorance of the English people as to geographical distances; so that the generally small maps now published led people to conclude that because they could place their thumb on Ardahan and their little finger on

Bombay, a Russian corps commander in the one place could send his leading divisions into the other; but the idea was absurd. That Russia would undoubtedly retain in Armenia all she could conquer during this war, he would not pretend to disguise; but how that could affect English interests he failed to see.

His language to me was very plain and outspoken; in fact, I must say this for all the Russian politicians whom I have met, that if taught to sing all to the same tune, they do it with admirable frankness and precision. It remains of course yet to be seen whether Russia will overstep the lines she so positively laid down for herself. If she do not, every credit must be given to the honesty of her policy, and the good faith of her speeches and her promises.

In the society into which I entered in the clubs, and at the meetings of the press, I gathered that the moderation of Russia is not to be counted on, and in my humble opinion I do not see why it should. The nation believes it requires for its development certain territorial acquisitions; but what Russia most yearns for is access to the sea. The success of her armies enables her to face Europe, and ask or take what she requires; *tant pis* for Europe, who knowing her, and what she was at, has not had the courage to check her before it became too late.

A general conflagration in Europe was to be deprecated; but it is a question whether the enormous development of a half-civilised and autocratic nation may not overshadow the liberties gained by smaller nations, and check for a time the gradual advance which freedom in thought and in action was gaining in civilised Europe.

It is to be remembered that a great revolution is yet to take place in Russia itself, and that Europe cannot hope for peace within its borders until that revolution has taken place. So that Russian armies are going forward as the pioneers of an advancing civilisation, whilst they leave behind them a nation struggling in the throes of a despotic government— a nation itself only just emerging from a barbaric slavery.

The situation now makes it more than ever doubtful whether Russian ambition is either justifiable or laudable, and whether those misruled provinces of Turkey might not much better have been left to work out their own redemption.

Of all the political leaders of Russia in the
capital, when I visited St. Petersburg, the one who
struck me most, by affording me evidence of the
amiability of Fate in so often pitchforking round
pegs into square holes, was Monsieur de Giers,
the " substitute " of the Prince Gortschakoff, and
temporary head of the Foreign Office. Whilst
getting the necessary letters and recommendations
for facilitating my sojourn with the Russian head-
quarters on the Danube, I had to call, on more than
one occasion, on him. With what a puzzled look
of perfect courtesy did he receive me; a certain
hunted glance in his eyes, as though thinking :

" Here's another who'll go away and say all that
I didn't say, and if I don't say anything, will hint
that my reticence is due to my incapacity; and
G—— or the Baron J—— will be writing to ask
what I did say, or why I omitted to lay down the
honest broad principles of Russian diplomacy as
agreed on at the discussion held as to the admitting
of correspondents to the army, and what was to be
told them."

He made himself safe, however, by telling me all
and everything, and answering every question with the
most voluble readiness, winding up his answers with

a little " hum," as much as to say, " I hope for my
conscience' sake you don't believe me ;"—on the principle of the Russian proverb, which says, " A lie is
not a lie if not believed."

One of the stormiest interviews which I have
ever had the honour of having with Russian great
men (barring one, with the Grand Duke Nicholas,
which I will relate in its place) was towards the
close of May last with the Minister of the Interior
for all the Russias.   At eleven on a certain morning
I was waiting by appointment in the great ante-
room of his mansion, in company with a dozen or
two of all kinds and classes, and on being ushered
to his sanctum perceived immediately that I had not
been happy in the moment chosen by me to present
my card to this keeper of the keys of Siberia.
Extracts from many English newspapers were before
him, the reading of which had not apparently afforded
him any peculiar pleasure.

Hardly was I seated when he broke out with :
" *Vos journaux sont infâmes*, controlled as they are
by a lot of Poles, Jews, and spies, who are endeavouring to stir up sedition and revolt in every
well-governed country in Europe."

I was so taken aback that I scarcely heard more

for the full five minutes during which he kept up
his tirade ; but I remember full well his saying that
" Had he had his way at the Cabinet meeting held
to decide the admission or refusal of correspondents,
not one should ever have been permitted to accompany the army, and not a single foreign paper should
have been allowed to enter Russia."

I deferentially hinted that with the exception of
one, our papers were certainly not in the hands of
the Jews, and that Poles were far too interesting as
a subject of study for journalism, ever to be allowed
to become actually directors thereof.

" *Mais que diable,*" said he, " all your papers
actually swear in the prints now before me that I
have caused a supposed insurrectionist to be shot
against his prison-wall without trial or judgment,
while in reality the scoundrel in question has been
pardoned and liberated two years since."

(This was in allusion to a romantic assertion of
the *Daily Telegraph* of a tragic fate having happened to some Pole.)

" Excellence," I ventured, " the very just irrita-
tion you feel—should there be no truth in this
statement—arises from the fact of your having in
your ' Bureaux de Censeur ' three very young men,

2

estimable, no doubt, but who knowing that your
Excellency's time is very valuable, only cut out of
the London papers for your Excellency's digestion
such portions of the paper as contain assertions or
records unpalatable to Russian ears.   You thus
only get matter for reading condemnatory of you,
your politics, and your country, and conclude that
these are the sayings of the whole of the English
press and of England ; whereas, had you time to
look into the paper condemning you on one point,
you would find it often just to you on others ; and
in all cases I believe you would find our papers
thoroughly honest and independent in their hos-
tility."

" *Oui*," replied the minister.   " *Peut-être, mais
en tous cas ce damné 'Pall Mall' n'entrera plus en
Russie.*"

He then seemed to feel a little easier ; but being,
as is well known, the most irascible man in all
Russia, he soon broke out again, this time against
the English Government.   Beginning with a polite
sneer against Lord Loftus and what he was pleased
to term his "*politique des cafés*" (a probable
allusion to the fact that that distinguished Ambassador had announced to Lord Derby in one of

his early despatches that, having had certain promises made to him by the Emperor on the morning of a certain day that peace was certain, he had learnt at a *café* in the evening that the ultimatum to Turkey had been sent, etc., etc.) :

" Did the English Government suppose that a power like Russia would forego seeking her just advantage because a weak unstable ministry chose to write uncivil words, and to back them with vague menaces ? Russia cared not one copeck for England's opinion, and the result would prove his words when the day of settlement arrived to test them. The reproach of the necessity of this war must always rest on England's shoulders, for had that country thoroughly supported Russia at the Conference the Turks would never have continued their resistance to the wishes of Europe."

This minister, General Timaschef, was the only one of the many Russian politicians whom I have met, who ever allowed the anger and the feeling of animosity against England which possesses them all, to peep out.

CHAPTER II.

ARRIVAL AT BUCHAREST—CONDITION OF THE RUSSIAN ARMY—
ANECDOTES OF THE SHIPKA PASS.

AMPLY provided with letters of introduction from
the Admiral Count Greig, from the Minister of the
Interior, and from Baron de Giers, to the Prince
Gortschakoff, Baron Jomini, Monsieur de Hamburgher, and to the Chief of the Imperial Gendarmerie, I prepared to take my departure for the seat
of war. I had had with me during my stay at the
Hôtel Demouth at St. Petersburg an old German
body-servant, and allowed myself to be over-per-
suaded by him into taking him with me. He was
the cause of endless trouble and expense, I having
to care for him and myself too in my earlier wander-
ings in Roumania and Bulgaria.

Six days in a railway-carriage is not by any
means, as a rule, a pleasant experience, but my time

sped agreeably enough as I made acquaintance with, in his own line, one of the most remarkable characters of the day, and son of a still more remarkable one, the Count Rostopchine (whose father was, as is known, the supposed instigator of the burning of Moscow in 1812). The Count was on his way to join the 12th division of cavalry, in one of the regiments of hussars of which he held a commission as second lieutenant. He was sixty-five years of age, and had given up a position of equerry to the Emperor to return for the war to service in the same rank in which he had quitted it forty-five years before.

He was a most eccentric character, and an old rip such as in my many travels I have never, since or before, had the good or bad fortune to come across. Brandy was to him as the mildest milk, fatigue an unknown quantity. He eat, drank, and talked all day, and would, if permitted, do ditto all night. An anecdote he told me of his father, reflecting on the British tourist of 1812, (who don't appear to have changed much since) is, I think, worthy of narration.

His father, in command of a corps, was, after the entrance of the allies into Paris, installed in a

house in the Place Vendôme. One day a visitor
arrived, whose card announced Mr. Jones.

On the owner being received, an undeniable-
looking British subject presented himself, and stood
for a moment contemplating the Count through his
fixed glasses, then said : " You are the Count Rostopchine ?"

A bow of assent was given.

" You burnt Moscow ?"

" People say I did."

Another long stare, then the visitor, turning on
his heel, said : " Thank you ; my brothaw will call
on you to-mowow at twelve, and the west of my
wewations on the four following days."

The brother called punctually the next day, but
his Excellency was out.

As the train neared the frontiers of Roumania,
signs of war began to develop themselves ; carriages
after carriages laden with men and horses rolled to
swell the number of the supposed 200,000 then on the
banks of the Danube, and poured rapidly one after
the other along the single line leading towards Jassy
and Bucharest ; by each station stood great piles of
bread, and heaps of shot, and shell, and cartridge-
cases, waiting transport, while here and there whole

parks of artillery awaited their turn to be forwarded,
and their guns to speak against the formidable
Turk.   Crowds of superior officers occupied the
first-class carriages, and those of subaltern rank the
second, whilst the third and the trucks were densely
packed with cheery masses of soldiers; those to whom
I spoke, took the war as a business matter: a necessity
for Russia, a *revanche* for the Crimea, a plan for the
opening out of new countries to add in time to their
own.

For the liberation of the Christian, as a liberation,
there was but little enthusiasm; Roumania was
looked upon already as annexed, and Constantinople
was the object avowed.   Everybody was very civil
to me, but I found that a sneer at Great Britain was
always to the fore on any opportunity which conversation permitted of veiling it decently.   One Circas-
sian amused me greatly on account of a vow made by
him of never speaking to a foreigner, owing, so he
maintained, to having been obliged to hold his tongue
for four months on a visit he once made to London
and Paris, in consequence of no one being able to speak
with him.   He had, subsequently to his visit, learnt
English, and was dying to show it off to me; kept
back, however, by his vow he talked at me, or to

me, through a brother officer. My great delight was
watching him endeavouring to stick to his oath after
his memory became a little clouded with the copious
libations of champagne we treated one another to in
honour of the deity of war, at the various buffets on
our line.

Arriving at Bucharest, my first endeavour was to
acquire all the information as to the exact number
and positions of the Russian troops then stationed
along, and waiting orders to cross, the Danube, and
from what I learned I can but conclude that the
number of men computed to be present on the
Danube by the correspondents of the *Daily News*
was far in excess of the number actually there, as
none of the regiments were up to their full war
strength.

This error was of great service at the time,
helping considerably as it did, to unnerve the Turks
and strengthen the confidence of the Russians in
their own power.

At the date of the declaration of war, Russia's
forces in Europe were divided into two portions,
one being called the " Army of Operation," the
other the " Coast Army." The first was composed
of four corps, the last of two ; on the breaking out

of the war three more corps were mobilised, and subsequently a fourth, thus bringing the whole armies in Europe up to the number of ten corps.

Each army corps in Russia is complete as an army of itself, and is composed of two divisions of infantry, one division of cavalry, pontoon supply and baggage-trains; six batteries of eight guns each to a division of infantry, and twelve guns to the division of cavalry, making a total for the whole corps of 108 guns.

On paper the corps should have 35,000 fighting men; the actual number of rations drawn for any one of the ten corps actually forming the European army never exceeded 24,000, one corps at one time only drawing for 16,000; in proof of which I offer the observation made to me by General Zotow on the 27th of August, after the defeats at Shipka, on which hangs a tale. Mr. MacGahan, the most talented of the many talented men which the Russian organ has chosen, and ably chosen, as its representatives during this war, woke me up in my lowly quarters in a stable before Plevna on a certain morning in August. I had a light barouche with four good horses swift and true, and Skobeloff

the younger having sent for MacGahan the night
before, and invited him to take part in a move
about to be made on the enemy's flank; our *Daily
News* man (as he candidly told me), thinking that my
light barouche would be more comfortable travelling
in than were he to mount his rough unbroken pony,
(his own carriage was away carrying despatches),
let me into the secret Skobeloff had confided
to him, and enjoining strict secrecy, asked me to
get myself, my saddles, and my horses ready,
and start with him, which I was nothing loath
to do !

Away then we went, about six in the morning, in
the direction of the Osma River, passing through
the village of Joglauv, where Skobeloff had had his
head-quarters during the few previous days, but which
now, owing to the movement of the night before,
was merely occupied by a small guard.   Joglauv
was included in the investing lines around Plevna, so
that when Skobeloff moved towards Selvi, as he was
then doing, he was obliged to leave a portion of the
semicircle investing Plevna completely undefended,
enabling the Turks, if they wished, to cut in even as
far as Poradim.   We overtook the baggage-trains
as we came down to the river, and there sent back

the carriage, mounted our horses, and rode up the
ravine which connects the village of Joglauv with
Trestenik, on the heights above Plevna. Here, on
the roadside, we came across Skobeloff himself, surrounded by his staff, lying on his back, watching and
waiting for his baggage to get through the heavy
sandy defiles, a task of great difficulty both for the
wagons and the field-guns which were accompanying the column. Had the Turks been aware of the
movement, they could at any moment have cut in,
severing Skobeloff from his main body of infantry,
which, having marched earlier in the morning, was
something like eight miles ahead, whilst his cavalry
was even farther away. This disjointed style of
marching was very common with the Russians
during the recent campaign, and, if ever repeated
with a more vigilant enemy than is the Turk, will
inevitably lead to disaster. Skobeloff left a regiment
of cavalry in his rear to oppose any sortie from
Plevna ; and after we had ridden for upwards of an
hour we overtook the rear brigade, and three hours
later reached the village of Karas. This moonlight
ride with Skobeloff, in search of his brigade, tried my
nerves to the utmost. It would have been all very
well poking about in the moonlight, up hill and

down dales which you don't know, within the
Turkish lines, and with a good chance of being shot,
if you were doing it in your country's service; but
when it is in a cause which one has not very much
at heart, and in the company of a general who seems
to be himself most anxious to stop a bullet if possible, I confess it required not unfrequent applications to the flask I always carried to keep myself in
proper trim. At last, very much to my relief, we
came across a Bulgarian peasant, who, on being
pounced upon by our Cossack orderlies, told us there
had been some heavy firing in the early part of
the day, occasioned by a sortie of the Turks along
the Selvi road, but that it had been driven back,
and that our cavalry brigade was then about half an
hour's ride from where we then were. We went on,
and very shortly afterwards were seated under some
trees around a bivouac fire, discussing some very
fair claret which Skobeloff had with him. Whilst
talking, a subaltern rode up with the news of
heavy fighting at Shipka, and MacGahan, without a moment's hesitation, rose from our bivouac
and asked me if I would go on to Shipka at
once.

I suggested we should wait till morning, but this

did not suit his ideas ; so, after giving a meagre feed to our horses, we mounted, and accompanied by the Russian correspondent of the *Russki Mir*, rode off in the direction of Gabrova. At the time we left, about one a.m., Skobeloff was occupying the small village of Ceret, half-way between Selvi and Plevna, and to the northward of the former place.

We reached Selvi about 3.30 a.m., and found Prince Mirski and his staff anxiously waiting news from the Shipka heights, it being then rumoured that the Turks had succeeded in cutting in between Fort St. Nicholas and the main line of Gabrova. Bashi-Bazouks were also reported along the Selvi-Gabrova road.

At Selvi we left our horses completely done up, and, hiring a little buggy, we succeeded in getting into Gabrova about 10.30 a.m., flattering ourselves we were the only two correspondents—the Russian having left us *en route*—who would know anything about the Shipka matter. MacGahan was chuckling with glee at the idea of having beaten Forbes, and I was delighted with having outdone all the others ; but our joy was short-lived, for as we entered the little hotel we saw Forbes and his comrade, Mr. Villiers, of the *Graphic*, making their way over the bridge in the direction of the Danube, a sight very trying to our equanimity, more especially to that of MacGahan.

Quitting Gabrova after a stay of two hours, we rode up the steep winding road which leads gradually to the summit of Mount St. Nicholas. The Shipka Pass is not of itself a very easily defended position, being a long, narrow, winding road, exceedingly steep, but commanded on the left by the Berdek mountains, and on its right by a series of saddle-back elevations which cover the whole extent of one flank for a distance of nearly two miles. As we rode up the steeper half, we met the wounded General Dragomiroff being carried on a stretcher to the ambulances established about a mile and a half in rear of the redoubts held by Radetzski. Dragomiroff was in good spirits, and his aide-de-camp, who had been also wounded, gave us some interesting details of the fighting on the two previous days, when two infantry regiments and a brigade of rifles, not exceeding 13,000 men in all, had held the pass, for sixty long hours of continuous fighting, against what was reported as 100,000 Turks under Suleiman Pacha. The aide-de-camp told us of the narrow escape he had had in flying, the day previous, from the Turkish advance. All the

officers of one of the companies of rifles holding the
extreme right-hand redoubt had been shot, and he was
sent to take command. At 6.30 a.m. the Turks made a
determined charge, coming on in much more massive
formations than modern conditions of warfare justify.
Having to pass over well-cleared ground, the short
" Berdan " of the riflemen told with deadly effect,
and continuous assaults were checked and driven back,
until past nine o'clock the same evening. About
3.30 p.m. of the day following, the Turks seem to
have determined to finish once for all, if possible.
Forming in long, loose, waving lines, three or four
deep, they made a rush at the outer redoubts, which
they succeeded in carrying. Panic-stricken at this
success, the troops in the redoubt, under this young
aide-de-camp, got out of hand, turned, and fled.
Seeing that it was useless to remain, he was following his men, when a bullet struck him in the
knee and brought him to the ground. Lying on his
back, with no pleasant prospect before his eyes, for
Turkish treatment of the wounded was then well
known, he was immensely relieved in his mind as two
ambulance-corps men came up and put him on a
stretcher. They had just lifted their burden, when
over the parapet of the redoubt close by, appeared

the red fezzes of the triumphant Turks. Thereupon
the bearers dropped their burden and bolted, and the
wounded officer gave himself up for lost, when behold
out of the line of advancing Turks trotted a white horse,
from whose back some Turkish officer had evidently
just fallen. The horse came slowly to the very
spot where the young aide-de-camp was lying, and
he, in an agony of fear, wrenched himself from the
stretcher, mounted, and, clinging to the beast's
neck, was carried safely into the broken Russian
lines.

Radetzski, as is well known, turned up at that
very critical moment, with infantry, mounted on
horseback, and succeeded once more in driving the
Turks out of the redoubts, and back to their old lines.

It is, perhaps, not inopportune to point out here
that the Shipka Pass furnishes a striking demonstration of the many valuable lives which may be lost,
by the too great confidence of a general after a temporary success. Radetzski, his general staff, and the
commanders of some of his regiments, having driven
back the Turks, went down and made merry not
far from Gabrova, rejoicing in the victory which
they thought they had so happily gained. This was
on a Thursday afternoon, and everything seemed

quiet in the Turkish lines; but hardly was it day-light on Friday morning, before it was found that the Turks had established three four-gun batteries on the elevated ridge commanding, as I have already said, the road leading up to the Shipka Pass. These guns at once began to sweep the road between St. Nicholas and Gabrova, effectually preventing the marching up of any reinforcement from the latter place. When the news was brought to Radetzski, the look of consternation that appeared on his face was something worth witnessing. He jumped on his horse without a word, and galloped off to the scene of action, followed more slowly by G. W. MacGahan and myself. We attempted to gain Mount St. Nicholas, but the bullets whizzed across the upper part of the road with such unpleasant per-sistency, that we thought it more prudent to dis-mount and stay under an embankment which offered some shelter from them. Mustering two battalions of a regiment with which Prince Mirski had rein-forced him during the night, Radetzski ordered them to advance over the open, and to storm the nearest Turkish redoubt. He placed these troops under the command of General Dorojinsky, with directions to take a battalion and a half up the

slopes, leaving half a battalion in reserve at the base ;
Dorojinsky carried out the order, but his men had to
pass over a wide open space under the deadly fire of
a whole Turkish regiment; and though they never
ceased their advance, they soon got into very scattered array, so that when half-way up the hill, the
Turks, charging down over the parapet of the
redoubt, had no difficulty in driving them down in
considerable disorder, and even up the opposing slope,
pursued so closely that I myself saw some of the red-
fezzed warriors scramble on to the Shipka road right
into the middle of the Russian line. These brave
fellows were soon bayoneted, and their comrades fell
back, but not before cutting off and killing, or capturing to a man, the half battalion of Russians which
had been left in reserve. Radetzski, though he had
practically thus lost two battalions, learned no lesson
from the disaster, but continued the old policy which
has so often led to the failure of Russian attacks in
the late campaign, namely, sending small detachments
of men, with no adequate reserves, against strongly-
fortified positions. All that day he continued to
launch battalion after battalion in the vain attempt
to take these redoubts.

On one occasion a battalion actually succeeded in

getting in, and holding a redoubt, for a short time; but no reserve being at hand, the Turks soon rallied with fresh troops, and retook what they had only a few minutes before lost. The weather during this terrible fighting was excessively hot, and the dead bodies, lying in the full glare of a burning sun, swelled and turned black with wonderful rapidity, emitting a smell that was utterly sickening.

Towards night, MacGahan and I clambered up into one of the Russian redoubts, and sat under the parapet, watching, through the embrasures, the deadly fight which was going on in the hollow and along the saddle-back mountains on our right. While there, I was struck by the evidence of the far-ranging qualities of the " Peabody-Martini " rifle—a close copy of our " Martini-Henry "—with which the Turkish infantry are armed. The redoubt in which we were seated could not have been less than a mile from the Turkish position on the mountain, and yet their bullets were whizzing overhead with apparently undiminished velocity, and men were falling from their effects a good half-mile farther away to our left. One poor lad, in running from one part of the redoubt in which we were seated to another, was struck by a bullet in the chest, which went

right through him, and buried itself deep in the
parapet beyond. The angry whizz of the projec-
tile was suddenly drowned in the heavy sickening thud which announces when one of these
deadly missiles finds its billet in a human body ; and
the poor young soldier, with a sharp shriek, fell on
to the carpet of empty cartridge-cases which literally
hid the ground, and gasped and moaned his life
away in a few seconds, amid the oaths of his comrades, who denounced him for bringing dishonour on
the regiment by his cries.

When night came on, we rode back to find
Radetzski, and to see if we could get anything to
eat. We found amongst all the officers, however,
nothing but a little hard bread and biscuit, as they
had been relying on being supplied from Gabrova.

While on the subject of the Shipka affair, I ought
in justice to mention the wonderful courage shown
by the Bulgarian water-carriers. In the middle of
the heaviest fire, these men, with their little donkeys
laden with water, moved backward and forward,
filling the canteens of the men. More than one was
hit; but they went on with their work with wonderful
pluck, affording a marked contrast to their country-

men of a better class, who carefully hung about out of range in the rear, and only sneaked forward after the firing was over, to pilfer the dead, Turks and Russians alike, and to bring in stray rifles.

During that afternoon I lost an acquaintance whom I liked very much. He was a volunteer, named Rieffski, a talented young fellow, occupying a very good position in St. Petersburg society, who, leaving a young wife and family, had shouldered the rifle as a private soldier, in what he, with so many of his countrymen, looked upon as a most holy war. As he passed me in the ranks of his battalion on the way to an attack on one of the redoubts, he gave me a cordial shake of the hand, and said, " If I fall, telegraph to my brother," at the same time giving me the address. Four hours later, having heard that he had been killed, I went out to try and discover his body, and found it amid a number of his comrades, the face already black from the intense heat of the sun.

It was very interesting to watch the faces of the men as they went into the fight. They all wore an expression as if they were gazing intently at some object beyond their ken—a fixed stare in the eyes and a nervous twitching of the lower part of the mouth, showing how intensely they were impressed by the fearful roll of the musketry, to which they were about to be exposed, and by the effect of meeting a continuous stream of wounded and dying, who were limping painfully or being carried to the rear. Nearly every wound was in the head or the arms, and all were of a very severe nature.

The high velocity of the small-bore bullet causes it to tear and shatter to an extent unknown in the days of the old smooth-bore musket, and the proportion of dead to wounded and of recoveries to those hit has been proportionally increased and reduced respectively. The situation of the wounds was owing to the universal fault in action of the Turks firing too high. All the wasted ammunition —and the proportion I should estimate to be greater almost than in any previous war—whistled far away into space, high over the heads of the advancing Russians, whose casualties would have been notably reduced if they had gone across the fire-swept zone a little faster, and stooping as much as it would be quite practicable to do without serious inconvenience.

During the whole of this Homeric three days' struggle—in which, by the way, I had nothing to

eat but a little bread, and nothing to drink but
water—the transcript of my note-book would be
nothing but a monotonous account of attack and
repulse, repulse and attack, with the ghastly accom-
paniment of dead and wounded, and of thousands of
corpses lying scattered over the scene of the struggle,
infecting the air, and swollen beyond recognition
under the effects of the tropical heat.

On the Sunday evening MacGahan and I determined to run the gauntlet of the shot and shell,
which were sweeping the road day and night, and
try and get back into Gabrova. Watching a lull, we
made a start, and happily succeeded in effecting our
object without being hurt.

During this three days' struggle, the Russians
must have lost nearly 4000 men out of the 8th
corps, the rifles, and one regiment of the 9th corps,
which Radetzski had under his command. But the
whole of this force, as near as I could ascertain, did
not exceed 16,000 men. As a fact, the strength of
the Russian invading army was during the war systematically over-estimated and misrepresented, with
the object, no doubt, of morally influencing the Turks.
It was pretty obvious that the Russian corps before
Plevna, previous to the last attack, did not muster

more than a fairly strong division and a quarter each,
in spite of the continued assertions of the Russophile English correspondents, that these corps had
left Russia from 32,000 to 35,000 strong. Radetzski,
before the Shipka affair, had had no previous
fighting, and yet he maintained to MacGahan and
me that his force was not stronger than from
16,000 to 17,000 fighting men.

On my reaching Gabrova, I rode on through a
portion of the road, then held by the Turks,
back to Poradim, and was asked to see and give
to General Zotoff (the second in command of the
Plevna army) a report of the fighting then going
on at Shipka. I assured him that the pass would
be inevitably lost unless reinforcements could be
sent. He turned to me, with an expression which
there was no mistaking, and said : " Mon Dieu ! où
voulez-vous que je les prendrai ?" and went on then
to assure me volubly, in French, that the two corps
under his command, the 4th and the 9th, had been
so weakened, that they did not together number
38,000 bayonets.

These admissions from two Russian generals
afford conclusive evidence that, unless their losses
in killed and wounded were much greater than

can for a moment be admitted, regiments, divisions, and corps must have left Russia far weaker than the nominal strength with which they were credited.

CHAPTER III.

MEETING one day in Paris a friend who had visited the Roumanian capital, I asked him what he thought of Bucharest, as I contemplated going there. "Well," said he, in reply, "you know they say that Brussels is a little Paris, and Madrid a little Brussels, my experience is that Bucharest is a little Madrid." My stay in the city led me to endorse my friend's terse description.

All that space will permit me to say of Bucharest is, that it is a place occupying a vast deal of ground—about four miles in diameter—for one-story houses, each standing in its own grounds, is the usual style of building; and that in it the observer has ample opportunity of contemplating the two extremes of European civilisation. The resident

Boyards, all of strong French proclivities and turn of thought, have almost without exception received a French education, and, as a consequence, the French language, French customs and habits, and French fashions meet one at every turn. On the other hand, the Roumanian peasantry—and there cannot as yet be said to be a middle class—in language, dress, and customs, reproduce pretty faithfully, in the nineteenth century, all the idiosyncrasies of the Roman colonists who, crossing the Danube 1800 years since, under Trajan, drove out the barbarous Dacians, and planted settlements along both slopes of the Carpathians.

The romantic history of this people—who were soon driven into the recesses of the mountains by the successive floods of barbarians that swept by from the Asian plains on their mission of European conquest—well deserves more careful study than it has yet received. Michelet and Edgar Quinet have touched the fringe of the subject; but the interesting story of the Roumanian settlement and fortunes in South-eastern Europe has yet to be written.

Long centuries of Turkish and Phanariot oppression and misrule have produced a state of things from which, under the genial influences of national life and free constitutional government, the people are vigorously recovering. Even now, however, the social condition of the upper classes is somewhat startling to the new-comer from Western Europe.

The women when young are charming; and when I say that they lose their beauty early, and their virtue much earlier, still enough will have been said to indicate one of the least estimable characteristics of Roumanian society. Amongst the peasantry, the women, thanks to the jealous supervision of their imperious lords, are much less loose in their behaviour. Both men and women are industrious. Land of extremely fertile character is easily attainable, and, as a consequence, though grossly ignorant of the first principles of good agriculture, the condition of the peasantry is decidedly comfortable.

One long street in Bucharest, called the Culea Mogoshoi, the seat of many of the best dwellings and of all the superior shops, would pass muster in a capital farther west. There is a fine new street leading out at right angles to this, called the Boulevard, which is intended, when funds are available, to be pierced as far as the Summer Palace in the western suburbs called Cotroceni.

This part of Bucharest is fairly paved and drained, but the rest of the city in this respect is suggestive of Constantinople. There is a fine new four-story hotel containing at least a hundred rooms at the junctions of the Boulevard and the Culea Mogoshoi. It is the finest in the place, and I am afraid I must add, in relation to the undisguised *liaisons* between its sojourners and the frail fair ones of the city, one of the most disreputable in Europe. Taking up my quarters here, I found that the Russian Consulate, in which Prince Gortschakoff and Baron Jomini and no inconsiderable portion of the Russian *Chancellerie* were located, was next door to the hotel.

I lost no time in sending in my letters of introduction, and the Prince sent me an announcement that he could receive me on the following day. I called at the hour appointed and was ushered without delay into the presence of the man who had played so great a part in the recent history of Europe. The Prince is a mild venerable gentleman of eighty, but wonderfully well and vigorous for his years, and with an intellect as clear as it is penetrating. In face, and also somewhat in figure, he is strikingly like the late M. Thiers; but with a beaming Pickwickian

look, when animated by conversation and especially
when relating any anecdote or recollection of his
long experience, which effectually masks the astute-
ness for which he is so justly celebrated. He
received me with great courtesy and kindness of
manner, and when I began to tell him that I was
desirous of going to the front as a correspondent, not
merely for some English newspapers but for the
Goloss of St. Petersburg, he interrupted me with
the remark :

"Then you have for your Russian chief the
most enterprising and least reliable of all the Russian
journalists."

I hope my late patron, M. Kraeffski, the pro-
prietor of that influential journal, will fully appreciate
the compliment.

"I am sorry to say," continued the Prince, "that
Russian journals and journalists scarcely hold so
honourable a place in our country as they do in
yours. Your papers give a fair and open support to
the party which they have for the time adopted ;
but they do not, like ours in Russia, endeavour
continually to stir up the unthinking masses of the
people against all government, as the *Goloss* and
others are continually doing."

I remarked that when I had the honour of seeing Count Greig in St. Petersburg, he had assured me that the policy of Russian statesmen was in direct conformity with the promises laid down by the Emperor in the celebrated interview at Livadia.

"The Emperor," said Prince Gortschakoff, with as much earnestness as he ever assumes, "has but one word (*n'a qu'un parole*). He has pledged it solemnly, and no success or reverse will for a moment cause him to change it in any way, were it even for the advantage of the country or for his own. In declaring war, the Emperor announced that it was for the Christian population of Bulgaria he was moving his armies across the Roumanian frontier; and not only is this the fact, but the moment the liberation of that Christian population from Turkish misrule has become an accomplished fact, the Emperor will sheathe the sword which he drew on their behalf."

"May I be allowed to ask you, Prince," said I, "whether the occupation of Bulgaria by Russian armies is not likely to lead to complications with Austria? And if you should not occupy Bulgaria, what guarantee would you propose to prevent the Turks, as soon as you have withdrawn your armies, recommencing the oppression which, as you say, they

have for centuries past made to weigh so heavily on
the Bulgarian people ?"

"Any lengthened occupation of Bulgaria," replied
the Prince, "will not be necessary, for we shall not
withdraw our armies until we have so thoroughly
crushed and humiliated the Turks, that though
Turkey may continue to exist as a people, she will
not continue to be counted amongst the military
nations of the earth."

Leading back the conversation to the subject of
journalism, the Prince said, "You are not the
correspondent of the *Times*, are you?" I told him
I had not that honour. He asked me then whether
I thought the *Times* at that moment represented
public opinion, and what gave it so much influence
in England. He listened very attentively while I
attempted, I am afraid somewhat imperfectly, to
explain the causes which have led to the prominence
of the "leading journal," how its liberal expenditure,
and enterprise in years gone by, had given it at that
time a priority in early intelligence, in addition to
securing the best talent of the day in every depart-
ment; how this combination had gradually secured
the suffrages of our fathers, and that we were
conservative enough to follow very closely in their

footsteps, though in regard to enterprise and expenditure other journals were now beginning to get on a level with the *Times*, and in the matter of early intelligence all, thanks to the use of the telegraph, were pretty much on an equality. As to representing public opinion, I said the *Times* could not always be accepted as an exponent of the opinion of the people of England, and I instanced cases of great questions on which it had rather followed than led public opinion. Beyond a certain stage in any question, I suggested that the *Times* might be taken as fairly representing the majority of intelligent thinking people.

"Well," said the Prince, "it has on the whole been very fair to us throughout on this Eastern question. Come in often," he continued, "and see Baron Jomini; he may be able at times to give you some inkling respecting political matters; but as for anything in regard to the war or what is going on at the front, we know nothing here."

I subsequently learned that was really the fact, for it was only on the repeated applications of the Russian Ambassadors at the different European Courts, "wiring" the Prince for information in regard to military movements, that the Grand Duke Nicholas finally acceded to his representations, and

telegraphed the result of each day's proceedings to
the Consulate in Bucharest.   Baron Jomini himself
told me that they were literally overwhelmed with
telegrams from every Russian minister and diplomatic agent, while they were absolutely ignorant of
what was being done south of the Danube.   I
myself on one occasion, subsequently going to the
Consulate, was able to give them some information
as to the state of affairs in the Shipka Pass, of
which they had no knowledge.

During my stay in Bucharest I had several interviews with Baron Jomini, the Prince Gortschakoff's
right-hand man, and Baron Stuart, Consul-General
and Minister Plenipotentiary at Bucharest.   The
former accomplished diplomatist is a son of General
Jomini, who served under the Great Napoleon and
wrote so exhaustively on the art of war.   Baron
Jomini does not inherit the paternal genius for
strategy and tactics, but exhibits no ordinary talent
in sundry other directions.   He has the credit of
being an admirable painter in water-colours and the
best *précis* writer in Europe; while in the suave
courtesy of his demeanour he stands out prominently
amid colleagues with whom the cultivation of this
useful diplomatic quality is traditional.

I had many agreeable conversations with this gentleman as well as with Baron Stuart, who, before the advent of his chief, had conducted with great tact and judgment the negotiations with the Roumanian Government in regard to the passage of Russian troops from the Pruth to the Danube. On one occasion during an interview with Baron Stuart, a note was brought to him from Mrs. Mansfield, the wife of the British diplomatic representative at Bucharest, a most intelligent, agreeable, and energetic lady whose subsequent devoted labours on behalf of the wounded in the National Society's Hospital were most exemplary and praiseworthy. Her application was for a pass for some young Briton, a surgeon I think, who wished to get to the front. After reading the note, the Baron turned round with a smile and said, " C'est une vraie Moltke en jupon ; there is no refusing her anything."

During one conversation with Baron Stuart, he made rather a remarkable statement of his views in regard to the future government of Bulgaria. He ridiculed the idea of a Russian governor being installed, but he insisted that as there was no educated class amongst the Bulgarians, they would not be able, even if autonomy were conceded, to govern themselves satisfactorily for some time to come; and therefore he proposed that the Exarch at Constantinople should be the supreme ruler of the Bulgarian provinces, and govern by means of the clergy in the different districts. I suggested to him that if such a plan were adopted, the Russian Government would take care that they had the appointing of the Exarch, and the rest of Europe would hardly be persuaded under those circumstances that Bulgaria was not being governed from St. Petersburg. He objected that his idea involved the appointment of the existing Exarch, who was already a spiritual potentate, and perfectly independent of Russian influence, so that it would merely be Russia installing an existing head.

I then expressed the opinion that no permanent settlement of the liberated Christian provinces of Turkey could take place except through the medium of a conference after hostilities had ceased, and that I thought, considering the ignorant condition of the Bulgarian clergy, and the ill-success of all clerical interference in temporal government, his plan would hardly find favour in such an assembly.

I had come out from England later than most of the other correspondents, and was therefore un-

provided with authorisations from the Russian
head-quarters, without which no one was allowed
to accompany the army. My colleagues, who had
arrived so much earlier on the scene of action, had,
after much dancing attendance between Bucharest
and Ploesti, got themselves enrolled *en règle*, and
provided with their own photographs endorsed by
stamping them with the Russian arms, and with
brassards, had all left for the front. The head-
quarters had removed to Zimnitza, and I should
have been liable to arrest if I had attempted to
follow without the necessary pass. Baron Jomini,
however, very kindly telegraphed to M. de Hamburgher, the private secretary of the Emperor, and
obtained permission for me to go down and see
Colonel Hassenkamf, the chief of the Military
Police, who had the supervision of all matters connected with correspondents.

Armed with this document I started from
Bucharest by the railway to Giurgevo. The
distance is only sixty-nine kilometres, but we were
nearly five hours doing the distance, for the Roumanian railways are all single lines, and the pressure
on them for the transport of Russian troops and
supplies was already so great that civil traffic was

virtually suspended. The train, though nominally
for the service of the public, was nearly filled by
Russian officials of different kinds, belonging mainly
to the intendance and medical service, with a few
officers hurrying down to join their regiments. The
only civilian besides myself in the carriage was a
Roumanian lady, who told me that she was a
resident of Giurgevo, and that with her husband and
two children she had occupied a house which on the
first outbreak of bombardment from Rustchuk had
proved to be directly in the line of fire. The house
next to their own had been struck by two shells,
completely ruining it, though the terrified inhabitants
fortunately escaped with no further injury than their
fright, and being covered with plaster.

She described her husband as having been terribly
unnerved, and as getting herself, the children, and a
servant, to the station forthwith just as they stood,
where he remained in a state of agitation until a
train started for Bucharest. They had then been
some days in the capital with a crowd of similarly
terrified fugitives, and though a sum of money had
been left behind in the house, nothing could induce
the husband to risk fetching it. Under these circumstances the lady, who seemed in the matter of

nerves to be the exact opposite of her spouse, had determined to come in person. I felt so much interested in her little story, that I offered my services as escort from the station to her deserted house ; but she told me a relative would be in waiting for her, and I was glad to see he had kept his appointment.

Before leaving Giurgevo that evening, I saw them on the way back to the station, the sole passengers, except myself, in a long deserted street, and I was gratified to hear from the lady that she had found the money untouched, and that though other houses close by had been ruined by the Turkish shells since their departure, their own still remained uninjured.

At Fratesti, the last station before reaching Giurgevo, I noticed the Russians were rapidly forming an extensive artillery depot and hospital station. A large number of siege-guns and field-pieces were already parked, and alongside the line were huge piles of small-arm ammunition cases just as they had been received from the New England factory for the Berdan rifle, and projectiles for the siege-guns, each neatly enveloped in a strip of Russian matting, which gave off its characteristic

pleasant odour under the burning rays of the sun.
The platform was crowded with officers, surgeons,
sisters of mercy, and nurses, each of the latter bearing the Geneva cross on a *brassard* of white linen.
Amongst them were a few of obviously gentle birth,
Russian ladies having, to their honour be it said,
nobly imitated that merciful mission, the initiation
of which will always be associated with the name of
Florence Nightingale. They were all in waiting for
the convoys of wounded men, who a day or two later
commenced with the passage of the Danube, to flow
back in ghastly procession to Roumania, only to
terminate with the cessation of the war.

During the somewhat long stoppage at this
station, I had an opportunity of seeing one of the
trains for the wounded, which was fitted up already
for constant use on a siding. There were carriages for the residence of the permanent staff of
doctors, nurses, and attendants, and a kitchen,
pantry, and store-room, so that during the long
journeys it would have to make between the
Danube and the interior of Russia, it was as independent of external supplies as a ship on a voyage.
Goods-wagons, had been utilised for the wounded
men, by securing ropes in pairs from the roof to the

floor of the wagon, with three knots at regular intervals. Between these ropes, above the knots, the handles of stretchers bearing the wounded were thrust, and they were then suspended as in a cot three deep.

An American surgeon who had come to inspect and report on such matters, told me subsequently that though inferior to the Roumanian organisation, he had been surprised to find how generally complete were the Russian arrangements for the war; but he pointed out that an immense amount of unnecessary suffering would be inflicted on the wounded during their transport by these trains, from a very simple expedient which had been used throughout the American civil war being overlooked; that was an india-rubber ring for receiving the handles of the stretchers and mitigating the shakes and jolts which in some cases materially diminish the chance of recovery.

Most of the Russian officials left the train at Fratesti, the few who went on to Giurgevo speedily disappearing on their several errands. The station, I should think, is about three-quarters of a mile in a straight line from the banks of the river; and the officials had already been unpleasantly reminded that they were within range of the Turkish batteries by shells falling all about the hospital, whose white walls were glistening in the burning sun a few hundred yards off, and at about the same distance from the brink of the Danube. Leaving the station I soon found myself in a long, straight street leading southward, with all the houses close shut and apparently deserted. I found, however, that some few of the shops had their doors opened a little way, and that their owners were pottering about inside in a purposeless sort of way, peeping out now and then with a scared expression as if they were expecting the immediate advent of a Turkish shell opposite their own particular establishment.

This street terminated in a sort of circus, which is the centre of the town, and from which six or eight streets radiate. In the centre is a queer nondescript sort of tower, fifty or sixty feet in height, which, dominating all the low, one-story houses of the town, gave an uninterrupted view over the Danube into Bulgaria, and commanded the town of Rustchuk, with its white minarets, which lies a little higher up the river. A Russian and a Roumanian soldier were up aloft keeping a remarkably faithful watch over the doings in the enemy's territory; for during the few minutes I observed them both men were staring intensely into the distance, shading their eyes with their hands, and on their report apparently a staff officer hurried up with a long telescope, which was speedily trained on to the suspicious point.

With the exception of a *café*, crowded with a set of roisterers of very mixed character, whose noisy merriment seemed out of character altogether with the deserted streets, all the shops here were close shut, and I hesitated for a moment where to go. I may say that up to this time, though I had heard some terrible stories about Giurgevo being in ruins, I had not seen a solitary trace of injury from the sundry bombardments which it had even then endured. Seeing a pleasant vista of acacias lining the side-walks of a street which, I saw, terminated at the river, for the masts of some small craft were in full view, I stepped into their grateful shade and went onward. Still the same utter desertion: closed doors and windows, and not a living soul, except a snoring Russian soldier, who was lying in the shade at the farther end, suffering apparently from a severe attack of *raki*—the Roumanian equivalent of the *vodki*—which he would have employed at home to secure happy oblivion of all sublunary cares.

I searched curiously for damaged houses, but found nothing that could be credited to Turkish artillery, and I began to think the Giurgevans undoubtedly frightened, but not much hurt. At the end of the street I found myself just at the boundary-fence of a nice little inclosure, planted with trees and neatly laid out with turf and flower-beds, running eastward along the river esplanade, a spot commanding a charming view of the river and the opposite bank, where one can imagine that in peaceful times plenty of that flirting and love-making takes place, which ill-natured people pretend to be the end and aim of Roumanian existence.

At the farther end I found a sort of *ronde pointe*, surrounded by seats occupied by a combined picket of Russian and Roumanian soldiers, who had sentinels stationed all along the river-bank. Close by an intelligent young Roumanian volunteer was keeping watch and ward over some Turkish shells, which were gathered into one spot on a gravel walk, and he pointed out to me that they were all blind, the fuses still being *in situ*. Then for the first time I noticed that a smart wooden refreshment pavilion near by was in ruins, the interior presenting a mournful scene of shattered mirrors, walls, ceilings, bottles, and glasses, while the ground all about it was strewn with broken glass from windows, and splinters of walls and roof.

On the opposite side of the river I saw a low-shore battery whose parapet scarcely broke the outline of the bank; and seeing at once from the appearance of the pavilion that it was this battery which had done the damage, I concluded that I had only to investigate in the direction of the line of fire to find out what other damage had been done. Curiously enough the houses, including one large hotel which faced the river just in rear of the inclosure, had so far escaped injury; but on going still farther back into the town, evidence of serious damage at once became apparent.

The largest building in Giurgevo is the "Gymnasium," a sort of superior school, which rises high above the surrounding houses. This has apparently been made the *pointe de mir* of the Turkish gunners, for I counted nearly thirty shell-holes in the exposed southern wall and roof, and all the neighbouring houses right and left, including the telegraph station, up as far as the central circus, were

more or less damaged ; some being utterly ruined,
while others had only received perhaps a single
shell. The Gymnasium had received so much
damage that it looked as if it would cost more to
repair than to put up a new building.

I made my way into the utterly wrecked
interior, scrambling over shattered desks and forms,
piles of books and writing-paper, and heaps of
plaster from the walls and ceilings, until the painful
reflections which such a scene excited was suddenly
interrupted by the snarling of a large, half-savage
dog, which had taken up his quarters in one of the
rooms, and appeared to look upon my entrance as a
personal affront. His demonstrations were so decidedly bellicose that I thought I should have to
bring my revolver into play ; but before proceeding
to extremities I tried the effect of launching a
shattered form at him, javelin-fashion. Happily
this took effect, displacing him promptly from the
mound of fallen ceiling, from which he was offering
battle, and sending him howling into the deserted
street, into which I was not sorry soon to follow
him.

The damage which then existed was serious
enough, but it was merely a trifle compared with

what the much-battered town had afterwards to endure from the incessant bombardments which subsequently took place between the batteries of Slobosia and Rustchuk.

I left that evening in a barouche with four horses harnessed abreast for Zimnitza, the comparatively cool evening after the tropical heat of the day very much diminishing the discomfort of travelling over the rough dusty Roumanian road. It was a most amusing night's drive, for I had as companion a young Russian officer of dragoons in search of his regiment, which he knew was stationed somewhere on the left bank of the Danube, who, what between grief at leaving a newly-espoused wife at Bucharest and the free recourse he had had to champagne, vodki, brandy, and other spirituous liquors, was in a decidedly excited condition.

He was, however, full of fun and good-humour, though some of his practical jokes on the unfortunate coachman bid fair at one time to leave us to our own resources in the middle of the journey. Being dissatisfied at the rate of progress, he bethought him of the gentle expedient of drawing his revolver and sending a bullet past each of the man's ears. The poor devil, frightened out of his wits, dropped

his reins, jumped off the box, and bolted into the darkness.   My courier had to go after him, and it was
only after a long chase and still longer argument
and persuasion that he was induced to return and
mount the box.

I arrived at Zimnitza about ten in the morning of
the 3rd of July.   I found the Emperor occupying a
little wooden house overlooking the Danube, with
his staff encamped around him in a large garden.
Each individual officer of the Imperial household
and staff had a small square tent to himself, with a
gilt centre-pole carrying a little flag, giving a
singularly picturesque appearance to the Imperial
head-quarters.   From the encampment the ground
sloped gently down to the edge of a cliff, at this
point some two hundred feet high.   Beyond lay the
broad river glistening calm and peacefully in the
sun, with a background of the opposite cliffs and
the town of Sistova with its numerous graceful
minarets.

I went immediately to M. de Hamburgher, who
took me at once to Colonel Hassenkamf, and in a
few minutes I found myself thoroughly *en règle* as
a recognised correspondent with the Russian army.
With M. de Hamburgher I am sorry to say I never

had an opportunity of any lengthened conversation, which I regretted very much. He made an appointment for the following day, but owing to the Emperor being at the crossing of the troops, he was unable to keep it, and I thus lost an opportunity which I all the more regret from the fact that De Hamburgher is clearly destined, according to the opinion of all leading Russians, to take a directing part in future European politics, as he is supposed to be the man on whom the mantle of Gortschakoff is to descend when that wily diplomatic leader goes the way of all flesh.

CHAPTER IV.

Since the capitulation of Sedan, no such momentous event has occurred as the crossing of the Danube at Zimnitza by the Russian army, on the night of the 27th of June. Great was the sensation created at Bucharest and throughout Europe.

I was not, I regret to say, present at the operation; but as it will hold a place in history as an event which must for ever affect the course of the future, I will devote a short chapter to a narrative of it, as given to me by Colonel Kamincka, one of the officers of the staff to General Radetzski, commander of the 8th corps, one of whose divisions, under General Dragomiroff, had been selected by the Grand Duke Nicholas to effect the passage between the cliffs of Zimnitza and a little to the north of Sistova.

The Roumanian bank of the Danube, nearly up to the town of Zimnitza, coming from Giurgevo, is marshy and almost level with the surface of the river; but around the straggling village dignified by the appellation "town," the bank is high, and Zimnitza itself looks down on a large expanse of mud and marsh separating it from the channel of the Danube proper, whose channel runs in close and deep by the Bulgarian side. This flat is of a necessity entirely commanded by the high cliffs around Sistova on the Bulgarian bank, and not offering any shelter from artillery, the Russians were forced, in attempting the passage at this point, to make it under cover of darkness.

On the night of the 23rd, the Grand Duke Nicholas had secretly left his quarters at Plozesti, and trusting himself in a small pontoon had crossed the Danube in the pluckiest manner, positively landed in among the Turkish sentries, inspected the ground, and indicated personally the exact spot where Dragomiroff's troops should first land. He remained for upwards of an hour, on this memorable

occasion, on the Bulgarian bank, without any in-
terruption from Turkish sentinels.

The Sistova side, opposite Zimnitza, is a sort of
muddy beach, some one hundred and fifty yards wide,
lying between the steep cliffs which rise perpendicu-
larly and the river, and leads directly into the lower
portion of the town.   It was on this beach that the
gallant Skobeloff and Major-General Yolchina first
landed the leading companies of their regiments,
crossing the rapidly-flowing thirteen hundred yards
of water which separate the flats of the Roumanian
side from Bulgaria, on the night of the 26th and
27th of June.

Dragomiroff's division had, as I have already
said, been selected to make the crossing, that of
Prince Mirski remaining in reserve ; two batteries of
field-guns were posted so as to sweep the opposite
beach.   And as the pontoon-boats pushed away at
the first breaking of dawn, these guns opened a
sweeping fire.   The Turks replied from batteries on
the heights, opening at the same time a musketry-fire
on the boats, and causing considerable loss amongst
the closely-packed Russians.   Only one boat was
however struck by the fire from the Turkish guns,
which have seldom in the late wars been very

precise in range, or accurate in bursting their shells.

By seven o'clock the 53rd and 54th of the line had effected a lodgment, and one battery of Russian guns was in position on the Bulgarian shore; and Prince Mirski, with his four regiments of reserve, was hastening over the Roumanian flats to get his men into the boats and barges waiting to take them to complete a work so well begun.

The Turks offered but very little resistance to the invaders on their first appearance; but an hour or two after the Russian landing, the position of Yolchina's brigade was made serious by a desperate attempt of the Turks against its advanced line of skirmishers and supports.

The Russians had succeeded in climbing by the various little paths that lead up the cliffs to the sloping plateau which conducts to the upper part of Sistova; and as at first they had but a thin line up there—awaiting as they were the arrival of Mirski with his reserves—a battalion of the enemy made a fierce effort to drive them over the cliffs into the Danube. At one time it appeared as though the Turk would be successful, and had it not been for the opportune arrival of a brigade of rifles, it is not impossible that a serious check would have been received. But it was not to be—Bulgaria was attained, and Sistova was soon to become a Russian head-quarters.

By eleven Mirski's division was on the scene of action, and one of its brigades had succeeded in turning the Turkish left, and cutting it off from the town and from its batteries, compelled it to fall back in the direction of Rustchuk.

At four the same afternoon of the 27th, a few Cossacks made their way without meeting opposition into the town of Sistova, and the first great step towards a successful campaign had been obtained. Already the few Bulgars present thought they were on the high road to their emancipation, and that the end of Turkish rule was near.

General Von Moltke, I am assured, had expressed his conviction that the crossing of the Danube would cost the Russians some 20,000 men. By a successful *coup-de-main* they falsified that able captain's prophecy, and certainly deserve great credit for the strategy which saved so many lives; 1,300 was the total of the Russian loss, a mere trifle when compared with the magnitude of the gain. The profoundest secrecy had been preserved, none of the military attachés knowing anything of the movement (with perhaps the exception of the Prussian, General Werder, who, as the acknowledged friend of the Emperor, was during the campaign kept well informed). In addition to secrecy a further policy was adopted, which misled the Turks most successfully : Nicopolis had been continually bombarded for two days previous to the passage, as though it was at that point it was to be made; whilst the Emperor further attracted the attention of the Turks by repeatedly showing himself on the high ground at Turno-Magurelle. An attack and passage was also made at Brailla, thus forcing the Turks to weaken themselves by extension of their forces, being compelled as they were, to defend a line of river of over three hundred miles, to check Servia on the one hand, and to guard the Dobrudscha on the other.

Although I am not fond of boring either myself by computing, or my readers with reading statistics, yet it is important to look into the number and strength of the Turkish armies, in order, if possible, to account for the remarkably sudden collapse of so great a military force—I don't say power—as

Turkey undoubtedly possessed at the commencement of the war.

On the Upper Danube the Turks were opposing the Roumanians with some 40,000 men; in Plevna there was a reserve of 11,000; at Nicopolis and Sistova, at the date of the crossing, there were some 13,000; Rustchuk was garrisoned by 30,000, and 65,000 were in the camps around Schumla; Silistria had 23,000, and the towns of Kustendji, Rasgrad, and Varna were occupied by large garrisons. In all there was a force (with every facility for concentration towards the line of the Balkans, and with a powerful fleet to protect its right flank,) of some 182,000.

Doubling this strength—had they known how to use it—was the fact that they were on the defensive, that they were occupying an easily defended line of country studded with fortresses, and peopled by a population that whatever a few agitators—for political or other reasons—may pretend, was not hostile to them; they could, by remaining inactive, compel their enemy to take the initiative; they could have defended passes which the Russians must have forced; manned fortifications which the Russians must have stormed; they had the com-

mand of the sea for supply, and two lines of railroad
for distribution.

They had all this, and yet one continued campaign
has entirely crushed them, and by a Power which
I believe was, and is, in a condition financially
and militarily nearly as hollow as their own. One
must, therefore, conclude that the reason why the
Turks—well armed as they were, well supplied with
every munition of war—so soon gave in, must be,
first, that "*Quem Deus vult perdere, prius dementat*"
(which was kindly done to the Turkish leaders),
and, secondly, that they had no leaders. This war
has not produced a single Turk—not even excepting
Osman Pacha—who could fairly lay claim to the
title of a " proper leader of men."

Suleiman, the only one who had a really effective,
well-disciplined force at his command, dissolved it
in the most foolish fashion by his vain attempts to
retake positions at Shipka, which nothing but madness—the effect of the old Latin proverb—could
ever have allowed to pass into Russian hands.
Osman Pacha himself gave proofs rather of cou-
rageous obstinacy than generalship. Moukhtar
Pacha was nowhere, whilst the Sultan, the Porte,
and the representatives of Turkey's pretty paper

constitution were "struck all of a heap" the whole
time. The foreigners employed by Turkey to aid
in its defence have not—whilst giving ample proof
of individual bravery, as might be expected of
them—raised their reputations, or produced from
amongst their numbers a Sidney Smith or a Dun-
donald.

Dissension, jealousy, and want of patriotism were
rife amongst the Turkish leaders ; the organisation
of the army was not such as to encourage and
develop the splendid fighting powers of the gallant
units composing it ; its generals feared the intrigues
of the stay-at-home pachas, and devoted more attention to countermining these than to checking the
common enemy ; but, worse than all, there was no
decided plan of action, no authority strong enough
to force on all a unanimous action of concentrated
defence !

When the Russians were over the Danube, there
was no one to insist in the councils of the nation
that the natural line ot defence was the line of
the Balkans ; no one in council strong enough to
insist on the evacuation of the Dobrudscha, the
fortifying and simply holding of the fortresses of
the Quadrilateral, whilst the loose, wandering armies

of Osman, Suleiman, and the others, made a united and determined stand for a defence of Roumelia.

Turkey was weakened by the hopes with which she deluded herself, by a belief, engendered by the past, that her existence as a Power was of as much importance to other nations as to herself; by the hope that, in confining the war to Bulgaria, which she looked on as a foreign country, its attendant miseries would be kept out of her own borders; and, finally, she was led by a certain portion of the English Russophile press to over-rate the strength of the enemy attacking her. Our press has deservedly gained a high character amongst foreign nations for the truthfulness and accuracy of its various statements; so that when one of the London papers averred that its correspondent had seen 280,000 Russians in the field, a Turkish general ought not to be blamed for believing that he has opposed to him a force somewhat approximate to that number, and not the half of it only, as was in reality the case. Should this general, then, be prudent, not to say timid, when he might have been bold—run away in order to live to fight another day—when, had he not been deceived by what he supposed was the statement of an impartial witness,

he might have stood to his guns and won—is he
to be blamed? And can a journal which has
served so partisan a purpose continue to be respected?

In July the Russians had in all, on the Bulgarian
side of the Danube, some 130,000 men, which, after
the memorable battles around Plevna, was diminished
by some 15,000 to 20,000. Fresh reinforcements
were of course constantly arriving; but so considerable was the loss inflicted by the Turks on
Krudener's corps at Nicopolis, and on the expeditionary force under Ghourko in the Balkans, that
these only served to fill up the gaps, and not to
augment the original number.

In their scare, the Turks never believed the
Russians would be so bold as to advance on Tirnova in the manner they did, placing themselves,
as they were, between two Turkish armies, with
Widdin on their right and all the fortresses of the
Quadrilateral on their left, except they were justified
in so doing by the possession of large forces. For
the nonce, at least, the Grand Duke Nicholas proved
" a host in himself." It was amusing to hear and
see the different foreign military attachés speak and
hold up their hands in profound military horror at

the thought that they, as accompanying the Grand
Duke, were positively doing, together with him,
outpost duty. That the Commander-in-Chief of the
Army of All the Russias should venture to Tirnova,
the very heart of the enemy's country, with a sotnia
of Cossacks and a regiment of rifles, might be *beau
mais ce n'etait pas la guerre*, and it certainly does
speak wonders for his pluck, if not for his sense of
commandership. But he had to go alone or not
go at all, as he certainly had no troops to take with
him. Zimmerman was in the Dobrudscha with
30,000 men, Krudener was near Nicopolis with some
22,000, Radetzski had a part of the 8th corps between Gabrova and Tirnova, the Czarewitch was at
Biela with the 12th corps, and Ghourko was burning
cottages with an expeditionary force on the Rou-
melian slopes of the Balkans. This accounts for
nearly all the troops that the Grand Duke could in
that month dispose of, as only part of Schahavskoi's
corps, the 4th, had crossed the Danube; so that
there can be little doubt that, had the Turks been
vigilant, and not over-rated the Russian strength,
they could, by uniting their forces on the Tantra,
have cut the different segments of the invading
forces the one from the other, or forced each to

retire, or concentrate on the line of the Danube until reinforced from Russia.

It was this desire for a flashing temporary success, rather than for cool productive results, that caused the disastrous attacks on Plevna, and forced the united military power of all Russia's European armies to be brought on to the field in order even to subdue Osman Pacha and the splendid troops he commanded.

Seated one day with General Krudener on a battery outside of Plevna, he gave me a detailed account of his first attack on that town, and proved to me in the most conclusive manner, by showing me letters and telegrams, that the responsibility for its failure could by no means be allowed to rest on him.

Krudener had with him for the attack on Nicopolis on the 16th of July, the day on which that important fortress was captured, all the infantry of the 9th corps ; but, as he explained to me, the whole of his division of cavalry was at that time performing outpost duty with the 12th corps before Biela. So that when the Grand Duke Nicholas telegraphed to him to keep an eye on the army of Osman Pacha, who was known to have been encamped at Widdin, but whose later movements were altogether unknown, Krudener could not fulfil this judicious order, for the simple reason that his eyes were wanting. He, however, maintains that he, as soon as possible, sent forward a regiment of Cossacks to occupy Plevna, but the colonel in charge, acting without orders, pushed on through the town in search, as he said, of Osman Pacha, whom failing to find, he returned to the Danube without bringing the slightest information in regard to the position of the formidable forces under that general. Subsequent information which came to Krudener's ears caused him to send a brigade to occupy Plevna; but this brigade, as is well known, was attacked by Osman Pacha's advanced guard south of that place, and utterly annihilated, while Osman's main force, on the 19th, occupied the town, and, without the loss of a moment, began to utilise, in the most skilful engineering way possible, its remarkable capabilities for defence.

The Grand Duke Nicholas was then at Tirnova. On hearing of the loss of the brigade, he telegraphed to Krudener—evidently in complete ignorance both of the strength of the Turks and the formidable character of their position—to advance

immediately and drive the enemy out of Plevna.
Leaving a small garrison in Nicopolis, Krudener
proceeded with three brigades and a portion of
his cavalry—which had been returned to him, and
was led by Skobeloff—to the neighbourhood of
Poradim.

Here he made a reconnaissance, which was very
skilfully performed, for it demonstrated the strength
of the Turks must amount to the formidable
total of 60,000 bayonets. Thereupon Krudener
telegraphed at once to the Grand Duke, urging
either that the 12th corps should be sent to his
support before the attack was made, or that until
batteries could be established no direct attack
should be made against the place, as it was
already strongly defended by earthworks.—These
important aids to defence seemed to have sprung
up as by magic; the Gravitza redoubt, which
subsequently cost the lives of thousands of brave
men before it was captured, was already dominating the commanding height on which it had
been thrown up.—Several telegrams passed, and
though we may assume that the exact position of
affairs at Plevna was laid before him, the Grand
Duke continued to urge, and Krudener to refuse, to

take on himself the responsibility of an attack which he knew could have but one result.

At last the Grand Duke telegraphed in words for which I can vouch, for I myself saw the telegram : " I am sending you Schahavskoi."

Now Schahavskoi was the commander of the 4th corps, which was at that time in the neighbourhood of Tirnova, and Krudener naturally expected that a junior corps commander would not come to him without bringing his corps with him. He was considerably surprised, therefore, to find that General turn up with his full staff, but with only one regiment and a few riflemen under Skobeloff. That distinguished fighting officer had left Krudener to proceed to Tirnova, and though he was doing remarkably useful work, was without any regular command.

Schahavskoi brought with him from the Grand Duke, positive orders to attack on the day after his arrival. Krudener, correctly foreseeing what would be the consequence of so insane a proceeding, energetically resisted the order, using the telegraph incessantly, and pointing out that as he had only 23,000 bayonets, and as Schahavskoi had only brought a reinforcement of between 3000 and 4000 men,

the chance of success against 60,000 Turks, already
strongly entrenched, was practically *nil.*

The final answer from the Grand Duke was :
" Attack, or resign the command to Schahavskoi."

" What could I do," said the General to me,
" after that but make out my dispositions for the
following day ? Those dispositions were as follows :
I directed Schahavskoi and Skobeloff to take the
troops they had brought with them and engage
the attention of the enemy on the left of Plevna,
whilst I, with three brigades and my dismounted
cavalry, attempted to force the position between
the great Gravitza redoubt and the town. Getting my artillery at once into position, I opened
fire in the early morning, intending to deliver a
simultaneous attack along the whole line at 2 p.m.
But at 12.30 p.m. I received information that
Schahavskoi had advanced contrary to my orders, and
before I was prepared to attack the great redoubt,
was actually close on the Turkish lines overhanging the left of Plevna ; but that his loss was so
severe that even at that early stage of the proceedings he was imploring me for reinforcements.

" Although I could ill spare it, I immediately
sent him a regiment and a half, and that force

arrived upon the ground just in time to save the whole of his artillery from being captured by the Turks. In order still further to support him by distracting the attention of the enemy, I gave the signal, against my better judgment, prematurely for the assault. My men went gallantly down the steep decline and up the opposing slope, through the Gravitza village, and made a hopeless attempt to carry the redoubt. Struck by the Turkish shells as soon as they came into view—for the field-guns in the redoubt were admirably served—men began to fall from the first, and their loss was rapidly increased the moment they got under the far-ranging rifle-fire of the enemy. The attack was repulsed with great loss, and though I repeated it four times, I could make no impression on the Turks, weakened as I was by the reinforcements which Schahavskoi had been continually praying for, whilst keeping me in ignorance that he was continually pushing farther away to the left, and thus leaving a large undefended space between him and myself.

" Seeing the utter hopelessness of success, I issued the order to discontinue the attack, but finding that my whole staff turned their backs on me, I reluctantly determined upon another and a final effort. The fight had been going on all the afternoon, when for the second time I received an intimation from Schahavskoi that if I could move round by the left we might then occupy Plevna. To do so at that hour was impossible, as, owing to the extension of the line by the edging away to the left of the troops under Skobeloff and Schahavskoi, our line was so weak and discouraged that I could not have got them concentrated before dark. I therefore made another final attack upon the redoubt, which met with the same fate as all the previous attempts, the troops being thrown into disorder and hopelessly repulsed before getting near the parapet of the work ; while the Turks, charging over the top, followed them up as they retreated, pushed before the victorious enemy, who might easily have converted this defeat into a thorough rout."

It is a fact, I believe, that a few Cossacks under Skobeloff's daring leadership did actually penerate into Plevna; but there can be no doubt whatever that the conduct of Schahavskoi and Skobeloff in their Quixotic attack, and in ignoring the orders of their commander Krudener, who was really a good soldier and cruelly ill-treated in this

Plevna affair, was excessively reprehensible. In-deed, I have myself heard Skobeloff declare that as a general he should always deeply regret his share in the transaction.

If Osman Pacha had been really a great general, something like disaster would soon have fallen on the Russian arms after the first repulse at Plevna; and nothing can justify his supineness in having allowed Krudener to draw off his shattered troops in the way he did. So great was the panic that it was only by great exertions—in which it is said he did not receive much aid from Schahavskoi and his staff —that he was able to rally the remnants of the corps he had led into action.

It is a notable fact in this war that Russian troops on several occasions, with little aid from their officers, and none from the staff, have had to trust for safety entirely to themselves; and it is astonish-ing how well they have succeeded in getting out of the scrapes so discreditable to those who led them into them.

CHAPTER V.

Having purchased a wagon and fitted it with cooking utensils, beds, lanterns, etc., and nearly filled it with tins of preserved meats, vegetables, and bottles of wine and brandy, I selected a stud of six horses, two being for saddle use; and with a newly-found courier (an excellent fellow, though rather too fond of his grog) started for the second time to the Danube with the intention of making for Tirnova, and, if possible, joining Ghourko in his raid over the Balkans.

My road lay as of yore through Giurgevo, and I had the good fortune to arrive there just at the nick of time to witness a little combat of the very prettiest between the batteries at Slobosia and six Turkish gunboats. I was well acquainted with Colonel

Exten, the then chief in command of the different batteries immediately facing Rustchuk, and paying him a visit at the little house on the banks of the Danube, which he in company with Colonel Bilderling was then occupying, he confided to me that he thought the night would hardly pass without something interesting taking place. Facing Giurgevo is a long low island called Ramadam, and above that again, opposite the port or landing-place, is the Island of Osde. Behind this latter the Turkish gunboats, ironclad and others, lay in waiting for a dark night, under cover of which they might be able to slip down stream towards Silistria, a movement they were compelled to execute owing to it having been telegraphed them by their spies at Giurgevo that continuous lines of Russian torpedoes were about to be laid both above and below them.

I elected to share the chances of the night, and whilst visiting the different batteries, selected by permission of the Colonel the most solidly constructed bomb-proof of the many on the line, and one immediately facing the island before mentioned where were hidden the Turkish monitors. A word as to these batteries visited may not be amiss, the more so as they were armed by guns made in England, or by English artisans of the newly-constructed arsenals of St. Petersburg. Each battery was very carefully constructed (its magazines deeply hid), and so well masked that the safest place in its neighbourhood was (to use an Irishism) within it.

The guns arming them were, as I say, the Armstrong, and those constructed in Russia; the latter also breech-loaders, and described to me by the Russian Artillery officers as being perfectly successful, the only complaint being with the percussion lock-firing arrangement, which is defective. The pride the men took in their guns, and their chiefs in their men, reminded me of our own Artillery; the cleanliness of the batteries, the careful building of the officers' tents, and the sanitary arrangements, offered a marked contrast to the different encampments of the line in which, during this war, I have dwelt; and I venture to suggest that when the future struggle between England and Russia comes on, our Woolwich men in the field line do not despise their enemy, as, whilst I have little respect for artillery *en gros* against works, I have more for it when used against men in an open or a wood; and the Russian field-batteries are very plucky.

Colonel Exten, Colonel Bilderling, two or three staff officers and myself, took the modest tea so general (and useful in its effects) amongst all classes of Russian society, and the dinner-hour having passed when I arrived, went all three of us supperless to bed. Whether or not views of coming glory so filled their stomachs as to leave no room for vulgar thoughts of famine, I know not; but this I do know, that I was hungry; and this I will say here, in order that Russians may amend their ways in future, their commissariat is always most decidedly lacking in whatever adds to comfort, though never allowed to be deficient in what will sustain life.

Dozing softly on a pricked plank, at about three in the morning I was awakened by a disturbance at the door of our house, and by the joyful exclamation of Exten, as he ran to open it. An orderly was there; a few hurried words passed between them. Exten seized his sword, I put on my boots, and then found myself stumbling after him along the marshy bank of the Danube, its murmuring waters on my left, and a dense white fog covering it.

From the quarters we had left to the bomb-proof

I had chosen was a walk of three quarters of an hour. We ducked along under the wide-spreading trees, our feet entangled in the creeping brushwood; answering at every few paces the murmured challenge of the sentinels hidden in the long grass, and stopping from time to time to peer into the dense white curtain of fog, hidden under which Russia's enemies lay. My boot came half off in a rabbit-hole, and the hustling Cossacks in my rear tumbled over me as I extricated myself—there was nothing, not even a correspondent, to be respected at that moment; the enemy was coming!

On getting into the signal battery (barely one mile from Rustchuk, and in which was my chosen cover), Exten, after communicating with the officer in charge of this battery, told me that muffled sounds of splashing wheels in the water mingling with the action of screw-propellers, could faintly be heard through the fog, and he thought that the Turks were about either to make a demonstration on the Roumanian bank or to try and save the many lighters full of cartridges, etc., which they were known to have hidden on the island covering their gunboats. He then explained to me that his system would triumph even to a certain extent over nature, as though he could not see his foe, owing to the fog, he yet could destroy him.

Each gun of the battery in which we were standing was trained by a heading-pole, through an outlying vedette, to a mark chosen on the enemy's coast; so that an object passing an artillery vedette marked A, and signalled by that vedette, might be missed, but could hardly hope to escape the other guns of a battery marked and trained (as B, C, etc.) in the same manner as was the gun signalled by the vedette A.

And this proved to be the case. I stood and heard the plashing of the steamers through the water, with the dull thud of the engines softened by the distance; and then saw the bright flash of our gun A answering to its vedette's signal. It missed, and so did B, but C sent a shell into a lighter carrying cartridges, and after that we wanted no further signalling, we could see for ourselves. A pyrotechnic display of popping cartridges ignited by a barge on fire, showed us four ironclads and six barges strung together attempting to run the Russian batteries. In one hour and twelve minutes from the opening of the first shot, two ironclads were sunk; one, taking a shell in its engines, ran aground on the

Island of Ramadam ; the fourth ran the gauntlet of
all the batteries, and what became of it I know not ;
but this I do know, that every one of the lighters
was destroyed and to be seen burning between
Rustchuk and Giurgevo for full forty-eight hours
after the first shot fired by Russian batteries on
this eventful night.   And eventful it was to such as
condescend to think, showing as it does the futility
of opposing ironclads to a line of heavily-armed
batteries.

It requires but a few men to work a gun ; it
takes one hundred and fifty to work a really de-
fensible ironclad.   The moral is then, never employ
an ironclad on a river ; keep it at the mouth, where
it can be sent to sea ; and from a respectable distance
(having become to an enemy an object almost impossible to hit) it can destroy a battery.   For it stands
to reason that a river affords to both sides occupying
its banks, and at war one with the other, the same
amount of protection, being as it is a perfect neutrality until turned by the superior of the two pos-
sessing it into a weapon.   And it only becomes a
weapon when you use it as such—not by its carrying, but by its upheaving powers : in two words, use
torpedoes.

If it is objected to me that banks of one river differ, and by that difference qualify my pretended neutrality of the water between them, I answer, nay, that a target is always a target; and be a bank high or low, close or far, its natural protection lies along its beach or its cliffs, and not in its streams; therefore, let batteries and torpedoes defend banks, and ironclads be reserved to bombard sea-coast places.

Before leaving, in this my narration, the gallant Colonel Exten and his batteries before Rustchuk, I think it well to tell of the great difficulties the Russian armies had to surmount in the early part of the war, on account of the treachery of their Roumanian allies on the one hand, and the robbery and treachery of the Bulgarians across the Danube on the other.

Giurgevo is close to the capital of the Roumanian territories, and much closer to Rustchuk. The Turks in the latter place knew, to the very close of the armistice, all that passed in Roumania, by means of their friends in Bulgaria and Roumania. They further knew all that passed in Europe, through the signals night after night made from Giurgevo to Rustchuk.

General Schmidt, the able commander of the lines of the Danube from Giurgevo to Zimnitza, assured me, on one of the many occasions on which I have had the pleasure of meeting him, that he had spent night after night out of his bed, in a vain endeavour to trace the red and white and divers-coloured speaking-signals exhibited from windows and other places in the town of Giurgevo, and fully answered and repeated by the enemy at Rustchuk. I know what the General's vigilance was, as I myself was once stopped for two hours by his cordon of pickets though well provided with the necessary passes. It was at a considerable distance from the town itself, it appearing that on this occasion he had arrested every soul moving in or around Giurgevo for a circuit of some eight miles, so baffled was he by the continuous signalling going on that night. Now and then he hanged a few stray night wanderers by way of example; but either they were not the guilty ones, or their place was for the love of pelf immediately filled by others, for the signalling went steadily on.

I do not care about speaking of the many other disagreeable traits presented by the Roumanian character, and may dismiss it by saying, that as a whole it is composed of a complete forgetfulness of all the ten commandments, added to a double dose of profligacy and covetousness.

Of their Bulgarian neighbours there is nothing more advantageous to be said, than perhaps to add treachery to personal cowardice. I am not one to judge a nation by the acts of individuals, but when I write what I saw, I may perhaps be excused for not being in love with this now-to-be autonomic race. I was returning from an expedition to the front and bringing in my despatches in the month of December last, when seated in my carriage I overtook a bullock-wagon carrying wounded. The mud and snow of a long journey had exhausted the poor brutes drawing it, and one fell out of the yoke to die; he was unharnessed, the wagon groaned on, on its dreary way. Scarcely was the poor beast unyoked, and lying on its side was striving to keep its nostrils above the oozing mud of the road on which he lay, when two well-dressed Bulgarian peasants rushed towards him, and drawing their knives, deliberately cut a steak from the hinder part of the living beast, never for a moment thinking of first putting it out of its misery. On our approach the miscreants ran away, though not forgetting their steak. A

Russian soldier passing fired his rifle into the poor beast's head and rid him of Bulgaria.

I took leave of Colonel Exten on the morning of this momentous naval battle, which proves distinctly to my mind, that monitors for river defence are absolutely useless; for river banks, however different, are each susceptible of defence. If a bank is high and steep, artillery is the natural means of defending it; if it is low, torpedoes are required. A monitor is not only liable to be destroyed at any moment by a hidden battery of sufficient power; but it can never move without the dread of being blown up by torpedoes.

A singular proof is afforded of the ease with which monitors may be driven off, by the fact that on the day after the crossing of the Danube by the Russians, all the lighters which had been employed by Dragomiroff for ferrying over his troops had been floated down the Danube, to form a pontoon bridge between the islands on the left bank and the Bulgarian shore, when two Turkish monitors steamed to the very spot chosen by the commander of the Russian Engineers to throw over this bridge. Yet a few field-pieces, partially concealed amongst the willows on the low and wholly exposed Roumanian bank, succeeded after very few rounds in driving them off, and they disappeared ignominiously from a point where, had they been able to remain, they might have done most valuable service to the Turkish cause. As soon as they disappeared down stream the bridge was thrown over, and the evening of its completion found me crossing it, on my way to the town of Sistova.

So many able descriptions have been given of this town, especially by the correspondents of the *Standard* and the *Daily News*, that it is useless to add another one, I therefore content myself by saying that, as in the case of all the Bulgarian towns which I have seen, its picturesque situation and brilliant sunshine on its white houses, mosques, and minarets, produce a favourable impression when viewed from the outside, which is rapidly and rudely dispelled the moment the traveller steps within its precincts. The squalid filth, the utter want of repair in the few streets that had any title at all to paving, and the all-pervading stinks which seemed tangible enough to be cut with a knife, I did see equalled in other places, but never, I think, surpassed except in the case of Tirnova, which in these respects occupies an abiding place in my memory, as the acme of everything that is intensely disagreeable.

With so little inducement to stay, I need hardly say that my sojourn in Sistova was not of very long duration, and it was with no small sense of relief that with courier, horses, wagons, and belongings, I found myself fairly *en route* over what is called the upper Tirnova road, and about commencing a survey of the country and people for whose emancipation so many thousands of brave men were destined to sacrifice their lives. I was struck at once, as every one must have been, with the patent evidences of the material comfort of the peasantry and the total absence of any indication of the grinding tyranny and misrule of their late Turkish masters.

For more than seventy miles my road lay over a long succession of hills and dales, very suggestive in their contour of parts of the Southdown country of Sussex and Hampshire, except that at times the noble swells of land were elevated almost into the proportions of mountains. The land is wonderfully fertile, and far as the eye could reach on either side, over hill and valley alike, were interminable stretches of rapidly ripening grain—wheat, barley, and oats, interspersed with still larger areas of the dark green maize which is so universally cultivated throughout South-eastern Europe.

Though the wattle-and-daub dwellings of the peasantry differ little probably from those which have dotted the landscape any time within the last two thousand years, they were surrounded by unmistakable proofs of material wealth. Cattle, sheep, swine, buffaloes, horses, and poultry of all kinds literally swarmed round every hut, and the people in their primitive but comfortable home-spun dresses had an unmistakable well-to-do air.

One is not favourably impressed with their faces and manners, in which they are inferior to the brighter and more intelligent Roumanian peasantry; but their industry is exemplary. Indeed, men and women engaged in field-tasks seemed, as a rule, so absorbed in their work, that they frequently never even raised their heads when we clattered by within a few yards of them. We passed through many abandoned and partly-burnt Turkish villages, with no sign of an inhabitant, except once or twice an ill-looking Bulgar, prowling about the half-destroyed houses, evidently appropriating any unconsidered trifles that served his purpose.

I had no time to examine any of them until I

arrived at Radan, a village close by the river Jantra, and about half-way between Sistova and Tirnova. It was past one in the morning when I pulled up my tired horses and pitched my camp inside the " compound," or inclosure, in which had stood a comfortable Turkish dwelling. Much to the discomfort of my courier, who was bent on eating, and rolling himself in a blanket as soon as possible, I commenced, by the light of the moon, and amid a circle of howling dogs, a tour of investigation amongst the ruined houses. The result was as saddening a spectacle as one can well conceive, for the evidences of wicked, wanton destruction were everywhere apparent.

Some Bulgars say that the Turks themselves fired their houses before following their retreating troops, and it was pretended that in many instances the Moslem masters had previously locked inside all their Bulgarian servants, with the philanthropic intention, of course, of burning them to death. Other Bulgars declared that all the destruction had been effected by the advancing Cossacks, who, according to all accounts, seem to have kept close upon the heels of the Turkish troops as they fell back from the Danube. From what I have

seen of Russian soldiers, both Cossacks and re-
gulars, I believe that, unless acting under specific
orders, they were not at all likely to destroy
villages, and it is scarcely necessary to say, that
without some well-defined military object, which
certainly did not exist, their officers would give no
such orders. In fact it would have been absurd for
the Russian advanced guard to destroy a country
which they had come to enfranchise, and to deprive
the army following them of the shelter and supplies
it afforded. On the other hand, the poor Turks who
fled were too much occupied in saving what they
could of their worldly possessions, to destroy, and
still less to commit vengeful acts on their Bulgar
servants and neighbours, who had it in their power
to commit terrible reprisals, more especially on the
laggards and the unprotected. I fear the verdict of
those who care to decide the point will have to be,
that all the ruin was caused by the Bulgars, whose
cowardly ferocity being stimulated by opportunity,
did not long restrict itself to destroying property.
I never had any doubt, from the behaviour of the
Bulgars themselves, that they were guilty of all the
devastations, the burnings, the plunderings, and
eventually of the murders and outrages of all kinds

against the Moslem inhabitants, which Turcophiles, both there and here, for a long while credited to the Russians.

The desertion of Radan was indeed complete, for not even a skulking Bulgar plunderer did we unearth after a pretty long search amongst the gutted houses, and in a moonlight so brilliant that no one could have got away unseen. The same absolute solitude reigned during the better part of the next day's journey. Plenty of ruined houses were passed, but not a living soul was seen until we neared Tirnova, when we met a few wandering Cossacks, and finally the rear of a baggage-train bound for the neighbouring capital of the ancient Bulgar kingdom. I was amazed to find, on my journey to Tirnova, that the Turks, in falling back, had left all the bridges on the roads absolutely uninjured. But my astonishment was immensely enhanced on reaching the broad and deep river Jantra, to find that the solidly-constructed stone bridges had also been left intact, though their destruction would have been easy, and would have caused serious obstruction to an advancing Russian force. It seemed, really, as if the retiring Turks must have been utterly demoralised, or else that they were inviting the advance of their enemy.

For something like eight miles before getting to Tirnova, the road winds amidst steep cliffs impressing one with their grandeur; and on coming within view of the Bulgarian capital, perched on a steep hillside, I was impressed with a certain resemblance to a part of Naples, where successive ranges of little white houses rise one above the other. The steep decline terminates in a number of scattered streets running into the great plain of Gabrova, in which were encamped, at the time of my arrival, two divisions and a brigade, with the Grand Duke Nicholas's head-quarters. From the crest of the hill over the town, I had pointed out to me the small house in the plain by which he had pitched his tent.

CHAPTER VI.

THE GRAND DUKE NICHOLAS—TIRNOVA, GABROVA, AND THE BALKANS—THE EMPEROR AT GORNY-STUDENA.

THE head-quarters of the Grand Duke Nicholas were situated on the slopes of a hill overlooking a great plain, in which were part of the 8th corps, a brigade of artillery, and a couple of regiments of Cossacks. His Imperial Highness lived in a tent divided into several apartments, and, barring the great heat from which he as well as commoner mortals had to suffer, was on the whole pretty comfortable. Every night he invited to his table such of the superior officers as were in favour with him, dining in a large room of a house close by his tent, washing his dinner down with many bottles of good old wine, carried with him at considerable risk and trouble, and soothing his digestion with sweet music played by his private band or by the bands of the different regiments guarding him.

I had a letter of introduction from M. de Giers, of the Russian Foreign Office at St. Petersburg, to Monsieur de Nelidoff, the accredited political agent and adviser to the Grand Duke; and on my presenting it and beginning to tell of the pretty little naval fight I had witnessed, he asked me to come and tell it to the Grand Duke. We found his Highness seated in an arm-chair under the shade of a tree surrounded by his staff. He bade me welcome, and listening with great attention and apparent satisfaction to the account I gave, questioned me closely as to what the Turks appeared to be doing around Rustchuk.

He then remarked that if I wanted to see some real fighting shortly I had better go round to Plevna by Loveca. He told me that large forces were being massed under Schahavskoi and Krudener, and that no doubt victory would crown his dispositions. He seemed to be thoroughly satisfied both with himself and with them, probably forgetting for the moment the check his right flank had received a few days back from Osman Pacha, and entirely ignoring that he had omitted to occupy Loveca, thus leaving Osman Pacha open, if he so wished, to retreat along the road to Sophia and over the Balkans, or should he be so minded, even come out and cut Tirnova off from Selvi and Gabrova.

In appearance the Grand Duke is a tall man, of good presence, very wiry-looking and stern, but with an amiable look when smiling. There is not much room for genius or great intelligence to lodge in his pear-shaped head; but he has enough brains for an Imperial Highness, for the brother of a Czar, and even for a leader of armies, did he but choose the right men to guide and direct him. Unfortunately he did not; such men as Nepochoitchitski and Levitski were his chosen counsellors, the latter his *ame damnée*, without whom he could neither walk nor breathe, nor sneeze, and to whom must be attributed all the earlier Russian reverses, the thousands of Russian slain now laying rotting on the plains around Plevna, and the hundreds buried in the Shipka Pass.

It was Levitski who planned the assault on Plevna on the 11th of September. One anecdote relating to that melancholy business will give a good idea of the calibre of himself and the other members of the staff. He was so careless or so puffed with conceit that he never even condescended to visit the lines or go over his proposed field of attack, but remained some fifteen miles in the rear, in the village of Radenice.

On the 11th, as is well known, General Zotoff was in supreme command; as chief of the staff to Prince Carl, General Krudener was on the right nominally in command of the 9th corps, though in reality only commanding one brigade of it, as one of his divisions formed the reserve in rear of the 4th corps in the centre, and one of his brigades of the remaining division was away with Skobeloff on the left. This arrangement was of course by order of Levitski, and yet that able chief of the staff so far forgot his dispositions on the afternoon of the 11th, when the battle was raging, that he sent an Imperial aide-de-camp to Krudener (Krudener himself told me this) ordering him to send a brigade to the support of the left wing of the 4th corps. Krudener replied that he had nothing to send, his only brigade being in position to attack the Gravitza battery. Another and yet another *aide-de-camp* came to him, and it was not until Krudener sent Levitski a copy of the dispositions as laid down by himself the day before, that that talented man recollected how he had disposed of the Russian force.

Nepochoitchitski was in his dotage, and did not improve that venerable condition of mind by devoting the best part of his time to courting Bulgarian peasant girls. The Grand Duke had really no responsible advisers equal to the occasion, and seeing that he is not a Grand Duke of naturally brilliant parts, is more to be pitied than condemned for the unlucky mistakes of the summer campaign.

Whilst I was conversing with the Grand Duke, Mr. Boyle of the *Standard* and an American correspondent named King joined us, and his Imperial Highness repeated to them what he had been saying to me respecting the attack he had ordered on Plevna. Mr. Boyle, on the strength of this, invited me to join him on a tour round to that place, *viâ* Loveca. I did not however go, as I was subsequently informed (and truly, as it turned out) that the Turks taking advantage of the omission of the Russians to occupy Loveca, had done so themselves. This omission cost the lives of many a gallant Russian, and threw back the campaign for full two months. Such an oversight is almost inconceivable by reason of its intense stupidity. Warned as the Russian staff were by the occupation of Plevna that Osman Pacha intended to hang on their right flank, and thoroughly advised as they must have been by Krudener's first defeat, that that town could only be taken by an attack on its left flank, they yet took no notice, but sat quietly at Tirnova, whilst Ghourko chivied Turkish irregulars over the Balkans, and Osman Pacha completed his lines around Plevna.

After my interview with the Grand Duke I proceeded, in company with Mr. King of the *Boston Gazette*, to the restaurant tent on the great plain already mentioned. We there discussed our movements for the morrow, finally deciding that daybreak should see us on our way to Gabrova, and thence over the Shipka to join Ghourko; for we did not at that time know that he was beaten and falling back. The evening saw me dining with a large company of correspondents of all nations at the rooms of the correspondent of the *Temps*, who elected to join King and myself.

Here let me say a few words as to correspondents. Mr. Forbes, of the *Daily News*, has so usurped public attention that the good work

done by others has been completely obliterated,
though many went through the same hardships,
and were quite as successful in their results as
was the fortunate one of the *Daily News.*   Mr.
Forbes himself, even, is apparently so persuaded
that he was the only one to the fore, that he
completely forgets the good work done by his own
colleagues, Mr. MacGahan and Mr. Millett—at least
if he does not forget he entirely (in the many self-
laudatory speeches which he has made and in what
he has written) omits to mention those gentlemen.
Great credit is due to Mr. Forbes, but that he
should have absorbed all the honours he has received without acknowledging or giving any honour
to the work done by others seems to me so unfair
that I cannot pass it over without notice.   His
colleague Mr. MacGahan is, both as a writer
and as a real correspondent, very superior to Mr.
Forbes.

MacGahan I have seen under fire at Shipka, at
Plevna, at Loveca, and at Selvi.   I know his worth ;
the sufferings he has undergone, not to write of
them for himself, but to gain information for his
paper, and to instruct, through it, the world.   Mr.
Forbes of course merits praise for his conduct

throughout a trying campaign. He is, I believe (at least, under correction), English; Mr. Mac-Gahan is American; both represented a paper which, to say the least, threw itself into the protection and defence of Russian interests, so much so that the Minister of the Interior of all the Russias said to me on one occasion, when speaking of the English press, and with all the bitterness that that sardonic old—well—diplomatist could use : " *Daily News!* oh! *c'est à nous.*"

Mr. Forbes had, by reason of the liberality of his newspaper, certain advantages which the able politicians of Russia wisely profited by; and whilst they laughed inwardly at the incorruptibility of the English press, and, consequently, the facility with which they could be helped, as a return allowed Mr. Forbes to take precedence of all the other correspondents. And on the 27th of June (the night of the crossing of the Danube), and when victory was well assured, allowed him to cross. At about which hour crossed likewise the son of the Grand Duke Nicholas, and the suttlers of the army.

Mr. MacGahan, being an American, and having no reason to curry favour because of the disfavour in which his nation (as that of England) was held, was able to base his independence of action on his previous hard services with Russian troops in Asia, and as a world-known correspondent of the doings of an Arctic expedition; it was also known that he was married to a Russian lady, who was acting for him (by translating his papers) as his co-correspondent to the *Moscow Gazette* of St. Petersburg, thus identifying him with Russian interests. His courage was above question. Skobeloff has told me of it, and I have witnessed it.

Of Mr. Millett I can say but little, as I have not met with him, his division of the labour on the *Daily News* not bringing him in the direction where I was; but I have been assured by men whom I trust that he was a good man and true, and certainly merited some little mention from the colleague whom all the world took it into their heads to honour.

As I am on the subject of correspondents, of whom, perhaps, every one is beginning slightly to tire, seeing (according to their own accounts) they suffer so much, and yet live through it all, let me mention one whose work was great, and his modesty equal to it—Colonel Brackenbury, of our Artillery. I met him only once, at Gabrova. He was then suffering greatly from the exposure he had undergone whilst with Ghourko in the Balkans, and was returning to England, so that of him I can only write what I have heard. But then, what I have heard was said by a Grand Duke commanding all the active European armies of Russia. The Grand Duke Nicholas said and wrote, " I have taken the general outline of the crossing of the Danube from the admirable letter to the *Times,* written by the English Colonel Brackenbury." Again, Colonel Hassenkamf said to me, when I, as correspondent of the *Goloss,* asked him for details of the passage (I missed it myself), " Prenez pour votre fond la lettre de Brackenbury."

There were French correspondents, and very good fellows they were ; and if they were not always everywhere, it is more the fault of their respective papers than of themselves. There were also Germans, who were, like the Frenchmen, kept on very short fare indeed, as to monetary arrangements, and yet did wonders. Our English journals, not even excepting the *Daily News* (which spent its hundreds by handfuls) often making quotations from the *Cologne Gazette,* which estimable paper allowed its correspondent twenty-eight pounds a month, including salary, for all expenses during this arduous campaign. It is true he could not live on it, and that his letters were often a little late; but he himself was to the fore, as were also his *confrères*.

There came after Colonel Brackenbury, replacing him in name, if not in worth, another correspondent —though I am almost afraid to call him such, seeing that he, so I have been told, threatened to kick any-body who would venture so to call him—Sir Henry Havelock by name.

"Qui est-ce Sir Havelock ?" said an old general to me once; "il dit qu'il n'est pas correspondant, mais qu'il écrit pour le *Times*, qu'est-ce qu'il est donc ?"

"C'est un membre du Parlement, mon General."

"Ah, un membre de votre Parlement! Dieu merci nous n'en avons pas."

On the morning of the 11th of September, whilst I was lunching with Zotow (that day in command), we were surprised by heavy firing on our left, and, leaving lunch, mounted. Coming upon the firing, we halted, and whilst watching the field, the chief of the staff was explaining to me in French, that Skobeloff, carried away by his usual impetuo-sity, had attacked somewhat earlier in the day than was expected; when from behind us a voice, in the most thorough British-French, broke out with: "Non, ce n'est pas ça," etc.; and went on detailing what the voice conceived the Turks were at. "Who is that?" said the Colonel.

It was the son of the gallant hero of India, accompanied by his *attaché*, who, finding little attention paid to him, rode away, to write a really good account of the battle to the *Times*.

The clever, witty De Woestwyn, of the *Figaro*, was also there, though obliged to leave early in the campaign for presuming to raise a laugh against the terrible Trepoff, Grand Maître de Police of St. Petersburg. However, he had all who laughed with him, and the only one who read and didn't laugh, was Trepoff.

Enough of correspondents. But just one word, to show how a minister may shut out a paper, and yet not shut out the wish for it. The *Pall Mall* was condemned in all the Russias, and had its editor ever fallen into the hands of Timascheff, Minister of the Interior, he would never have survived to give a detailed experience of the horrors of an inquisition. Well, the *Pall Mall* was condemned; yet one afternoon, sitting in my room in the Hôtel du Boulevard,

8—2

Bucharest, in company with Colonel T——, one of the Emperor's aides-de-camp, he spied amongst my papers the condemned *Pall Mall*. Rushing at it, he shook it as an old friend, and having devoured its contents, said :

"Stanley, send it to me in future, when you have done with it."

"You'll be hanged if they catch you with it," said I to him.

"Que m'importe ?" he replied. "Il fait si bon de lire la vérité quelquefois."

It was the 31st of July when I arrived at Gabrova, and the situation of the Prince Mirski, then in command of the few troops stationed at that place, was becoming hourly more critical and interesting. He was then awaiting news of the great battle daily and hourly expected to come off near Plevna, a short account of which I have already given in an earlier chapter, as told to me by Krudener, its unfortunate director.

What a lovely country leads to Gabrova ; and what a filthy smelling hole Gabrova is, or was ! It may have become purified since, under the beneficent sway of the benign generals of the Czar—good generals and good fellows as fellows they are, especially towards one who can "write about 'em, and talk about 'em, and tell about 'em ;" but Heaven keep me from their care were I a Turkish refugee or a Bulgarian peasant. Not that they would go out of their way to do either of these any harm, but that they would laugh at the idea of going out of their way to do them any good. The Russian troops never pillage, and certainly do not massacre; but, for all that, they are no more beloved by the Bulgarians than they are by the Poles. The delivered look on their deliverers very suspiciously, and verily, I believe, regret the days when they were obliged to employ all the ingenuity of their rascally nature in dodging Turkish zaptiehs gathering taxes. I haven't a stolen pony embittering my reminiscences, as, according to Mr. Freeman, Mr. Forbes had. But I bought horses of them, and they made me pay long bills; and I suffered from such continuous deceptions, that I always felt a sort of calm satisfaction, when speaking to a Russian warrior, in thinking that he, and not I, was fighting for the deliverance of this white-livered Bulgarian race. I believe, and I say it conscientiously, that the atrocities committed on Russians, Turks, and even Bulgars, were mostly committed by Bulgarians, that

the Bashi-Bazouks were, to make free with a bull,
Bulgarian Bashi-Bazouks.   Many a time, I feel
assured, have I saved my life and turned a Bulgarian
enemy into a Bulgarian friend, by the carrying of
my revolver in my hand.   I remember once (and
though it is not to my credit, I'll tell it), I lost my
temper; it was the day after the battle of the
25th in the Shipka Pass, and an order had been
given to hold all ready for evacuating Gabrova.
The Bulgarians, never thinking of arming in their
own defence, were wringing their hands, and cursing
in their fear their deliverers.   I was very tired and
thirsty, having passed all the Sunday night leading
my poor tired horse from the summit of the Shipka
Pass to the environs of Gabrova.

Seeing a house, I went to its porch, and asked a
drink of water.   The man cursed me for a Russian.
I struck him over the head with the butt-end of my
riding-whip.   He brought me out the water on his
knees! The results of oppression, some will say.   It
is not so.   At the hour of their deliverance they
were a white-livered *prosperous* set of curs, and a
prosperous white-livered set of curs they will remain.

After Shipka I returned to Selvi, where Prince
Mirski had his quarters in the cleanest house

that it could afford. For this Prince, though you might point him out as the pluckiest, was, even in the battle-fields of Bulgaria, always the daintiest and the most dandified of all the Russian dandy generals. And, good fighters as they undoubtedly are, Russian generals (excepting those of German origin, who of course cling to old tradition) are a neat and dandy race. I am classing them apart, and as a race distinct, advisedly, for though not Heaven-born, they are Czar-born. None can hope for the rank of leaders of Russian armies unless their fathers have lost Russian armies before, or at least are qualified by some ancestor having received an Imperial embrace, or a mandate for Siberia. I do not wish to make reflections, but still I fear that this limitation in choice had somewhat to do with the heavy losses of Russia's summer campaign.

On the three occasions on which I dined with General Prince Mirski, I was struck with admiration on the first at the tranquillity with which he supported the trial of a leg broken (I believe by a splinter from a shell) at the knee-joint; on the second occasion by the equanimity with which he supported the loss of one brigade and one regiment (out of a division), added to the loss of a position, the retaining of which was at that moment of vital importance to the whole Russian army; and thirdly and lastly, the kindly way he looked at the order of the Emperor, suggesting that he should retire from the command of his remaining regiment, and recruit his health at Bucharest. So thoughtful of the Emperor, said he to me in confidence (for the benefit of my paper the *Goloss*). Eating as I was at the moment the juiciest beefsteaks, when beefsteaks even without juice were rare, I thought it was far from thoughtful of the Emperor to remove the best table from the front.

Ah me, what a lot of lies and massacres I swallowed at Selvi. Every other man I met was a Bulgarian refugee from Loveca, whose wife and family had first been ravished and pillaged by Turks, and then pillaged and ravaged (if there is such a word) by Cossacks—five hundred of them in round numbers—all murdered! all massacred! And yet when the gallant Skobeloff and Immeretinski, the chief of the 2nd division, took Loveca some three weeks later, and I went into that town to confirm the horrors I had been told of, I found all that massacred five hundred alive and cheerful.

Well, I left the good beefsteaks of the hospitable Prince Mirski, regretting them, and also foolishly, not knowing the ways of Russian success, regretting the apparent disgrace of a charming fellow (so rare in these degenerate days). Alas for Russia, there was no pity needed, as there was no disgrace; it was only a brigade and a regiment lost—let us say roughly some eight thousand men—of which a quarter were dead, a quarter were prisoners, and one half were demoralised; but then the General, a Russian Prince, was left; his leg, thanks to the beneficent order of his beneficent Czar, was by rest restored to him. And when success returned to the Russian arms, his division was given back to him likewise.

Towards the middle of August, whilst returning towards the south and passing through Gorny Studen, I was a witness of the arrival there of the Emperor of all the Russias, coming from Biela, accompanied by a large and brilliant staff, conspicuous amongst whom was General Ghourko, from the Balkans, with renown crowning him, and defeat checking that renown; but the order of that day was a kindly smile on the Imperial face, so that from a doubtful hero he passed at once into a full-blown and successful one.

General Ghourko was a General of one of the divisions of the Imperial Guard of Russia. Previous to the crossing of the Danube, it was determined that, once that great object attained, a strong advance-guard should be pushed forward into the very centre of the Turkish positions in Bulgaria—in the first place, in order to divide them; in the second, to obtain, if possible, some of the moral effects and the material results obtained by the Uhlans in their rapid action during the Franco-German war.

Head-quarters were divided in their opinion as to who should have command of this expedition, as it was of a nature requiring prudence combined with dash, qualities not easy to be found amongst the generals commanding. One half were minded to have General Skobeloff, known to be of a character equal to the requirements of the case, and of a prudence consequent on his Jewish descent. The other half were opposed to his selection.

Skobeloff was not, and is not, of the aristocratic party—or rather, again, of the Court party, between whom and the true aristocrat of Russia there is a deep feud—in fact, he was of no party at all; he was simply a man of energy, a man of talent, a man who was sure to succeed. But his success would be offensive, so that it was deemed better, more prudent, to place in command of this expeditionary force which has startled all Europe by its achievements, and made all Europe laugh at its results, General Ghourko. His orders were—*nil.* His instructions were—*nil.* He was to take a body of men, who were to take their lives in their hands, and they were to go as far as they could go, as straight as circumstances and the Turks would allow them to go.

So the Danube was crossed; and General Ghourko went wherever the most enterprising amongst his Cossacks led him, coming as he was into a land in which was milk, and in which was, if not honey, something even somewhat more substantial —fields of glowing corn, rivulets of running water, clear as crystal, good stout beeves, young pigs wanting only knife and fork, and mutton without even the asking.

So on kept the advance-guard, nominally under charge of General Ghourko, in reality running forward of itself; on they kept, and before them the Turkish occupants ran from the Turkish villages, burning them as they went ; and the Turcophiles in England swore heartily that the Russian burnt the village in which the Mussulman lived.

Tirnova was entered without a blow ; half a dozen Cossacks rode through a defile that half a dozen Turks could have held against half a dozen thousand Russians ; but the Turk was disorganised.

He saw the Russians in myriads everywhere— every Cossack was to him a thousand pitiless foes ; so he fled ; and our quiet Cossack, poking himself along, thought it was all very jolly—good quarters, plenty to eat, very little Turk, and then only his back—followed after.

Then General Ghourko's advance-guard entered Tirnova, and garlands of roses were hung across, or rather held across, the streets ; and in single file the conquering army, consisting of three Cossacks and a sergeant, marched in, wondering how they were to get out again. And the people stretched their necks for four days towards the north, awaiting the main body, which finally came and saw, having already conquered, and then threaded its way by the compass south, a little westerly, towards Adrianople, arriving with 12,000 men at Gabrova on the

13th or so of July, winding its way without opposition over otherwise impassable passes, storming Kazanlik and driving its defenders back towards the Shipka Pass and fort, already threatened by the advance of General Skobeloff the elder on July the 18th.

Shipka was, as all know, taken, and twenty-five Russians dead, horribly mutilated, after being taken prisoners, found therein. Eski Zagra was attacked, and Ghourko and his 12,000 made themselves felt.

One day, when at Gorny Studen, where I had hidden myself in a hovel, and in that hovel was glad to be sheltered, I passed the evening listening, through means of my interpreter, to the details (given by the mother of the bairns then hanging about me, and whom I had won over by the gift of an English halfpenny, hiding itself somewhere in one of my pockets), of what her sufferings had been as the Turkish troops passed there in their flight from Sistova in the early days of July; how one of her little ones ran out from his hiding-place to drive away the dogs from a soldier forcing his way over the hedge of their little six-foot-square plantation, and how the Turk, turning his attention from the dogs to the baby running at them, shot the little one through the body.

There was deep sorrow and disgust throughout the Russian armies. Again had a fierce attack been made on Plevna, only to meet with the same disastrous repulse as on the first occasion. The hospitals were crowded with wounded and dying, the hearts of the soldiers were weary within them, the heat of the sun was overpowering, the promised reinforcements were arriving but slowly. Everywhere the Turkish arms seemed to be successful.

Ghourko had been forced to retire from Shipka, the village of which name was occupied by Suleiman Pacha ; Krudener and Schahavskoi had, as I have already said, met with a bloody repulse at Plevna ; Radetzski was threatened at Gabrova, and the Grand Duke himself had had to retire from Tirnova. The army of the Czarewitch was remaining inactive around Biela, threatened in its communications, and fearful of being outflanked. And H. I. Majesty the Czar was said to be suffering greatly both mentally and bodily, a fact of which I myself was a witness ; for when at Gorny Studen on the 11th of August, the day of his entry into that place from Biela, I was much struck by the change anxiety and active trouble had wrought on him since I had seen him leaving the Alexandrina station near the Tsarke-Seloë Palace some two or three months before.

Men are naturally impressed by surroundings, hence the divinity which doth hedge about a king ; but a battle-field, a badly-constructed tent, a wet day, and a highly-smelling camp, are great levellers. Notwithstanding that all these evils were heaped together on the day that I saw the Emperor, he struck me first as being a superior man ; secondly, as being every inch a king. He has both the reserve attached to his position and a kindly temper, which without ever trenching on *bonhomie*, lends a charm to his rather melancholy disposition—a disposition easily accounted for if the prophecy in regard to the Romanoff family has any weight with him ; for that prophecy runs that "no Romanoff doth the years of sixty see." However, as the years of Pio Nono overshot those of Peter, may the present Emperor live to sign a treaty of peace as agreeable to England as was that of 1856 !

What dirty little hovels every one lived in at Gorny Studen ; but my fate was not to be allowed even to live in one of these squalid dens beyond the second night of my arrival. Politely and civilly, yet imperatively, came a staff officer to me, and invited me to clear out.   My chosen hut (full of fleas and vermin less mentionable to ears polite) had been selected as a lodging for an Imperial Highness, a nephew of the Emperor, the young Duke de Leuchtenberg (who was afterwards killed by a bullet through the temple whilst gallantly leading a scouting-party.   To confess only the simple truth, they didn't spare themselves, these sons and nephews of Russia's greatest).

I turned out under the trees, and while pitching my camp the young Duke came to me, hearing that I had been turned out on his account, and excused himself on the plea of illness.   I could not but admire him for his thoughtful kindness of manner, and was a sincere mourner on the first day of November when I witnessed the carrying back of his remains to his native country.

At Gorny Studen the Emperor occupied a two-storied house perched on the edge of a plateau, separated by a deep ravine from the head-quarters of the Commander-in-Chief the Grand Duke Nicholas, who had quarters in the courtyard of a farm over-looking a wide plain very similar to the one at Tirnova.

The position was well chosen, as the roads from Biela, Sistova, Tirnova, and in fact all the communications then open to the Russian army, enclosed as they were on both flanks, centred in this place; and the ground being high, with proper sanitary arrangements, the health of the troops might have been good, but sanitary arrangements were always neglected. Latrines were dug for the use of the soldiers, but they were seldom used, and their use was never enforced. Even on the day of the entry of the Czar into the camp, the ground was in so disgusting a condition that his white charger sniffed the air daintily, and showed some disinclination to advance.

The regimental system of the Russian army is essentially faulty. The subalterns are fairly good officers although now rather a mean class of men socially, but from the captain upwards all is bad. Battalion commanders are as a rule helpless and worthless; and the colonels are chosen from the staff or by the influence of family connections, without the slightest regard to their fitness for the responsible duties they would have to perform in modern warfare against a European enemy.

9

CHAPTER VII.

THE TURKISH SORTIE—ATTACK ON SGALINÇA—THE TAKING OF LOVECA—PREPARATIONS FOR THE THIRD ATTACK ON PLEVNA.

SHORTLY afterwards I returned to Bucharest, driving into that charming little city of iniquity, which for smells beats Buenos Ayres, for dirt is equal to Constantinople, and for immorality rivals all the capitals of Europe put together. I drove in with pleasure, leaving as I was a country morally lower, though in another way, than the capital of the country to which I was returning; and I left that capital to return to the country I had left with the same pleasurable feelings that a man feels when disgusted with two evils, he falls back on the lesser.

Bulgaria is better than Roumania. Bulgarian men are mean and selfish, cowardly and traitors to all who are not Bulgar; but they have a sense of honour left, since they protect and honour their women—I would almost say cherish them, if such a feeling could be conceived to enter the souls of such a race. On the other hand, the Roumanian men take a pleasure in making the mothers of their sons what they are; and strut, and swell an inch taller on the presumption that they each and all are the sons of many fathers.

Ye gods! what brutal races they are; and yet Europe is about to plunge into a war—some one hundred million of beings are to have *their* interests jeopardised—in order to settle the limits of four millions of degenerate yellow-skinned people, and whether they shall or shall not have an autonomy, of which they know not even the first principle, and are ignorant of the very meaning of the word.

I went back to Poradim after a four-and-twenty hours' rest in Bucharest, and in order that the reader should not suppose that the going back to Poradim was one of those little trifling matters— such as, for instance, a comfortable journey in the Scotch mail to Edinburgh, or by the 8.25 to Ireland, with the help of sleeping-cars—let me give some details as to what the road really was between

Bucharest in Roumania and Poradim before Plevna. First then, leaving my hotel, I had a long drive to a railway station, then I had to find a seat in a train waiting, not for the guard, as in England, but in order to know if the Turks were shying the missiles of their Krupp guns on to the station to which she was destined. Supposing me then to be sufficiently fortunate, and the train to start, I, or rather my train lingers along the road, screaming and puffing, first going back of itself, then being put back by the different clashing Russo-Roumanian authorities directing its transit; at last we get into Giurgevo (its destination and rest). My real troubles begin; I have left there a courier, a wagon, and four horses. If I find my courier (a problem in itself), I find him drunk, or if sober, the horses incapable; it never mattered which, but the result was always the same, I could not go on that day. Well, I wanted to go on that day, and not on the morrow, so I had to open my purse-strings; and I went, and so did my money.

Finally, then, I have my horses in, my driver and courier and cook perched up in front, whilst I lay luxuriously behind, in vain trying to find a comfortable rest for my legs, and away we go.

All is silent for the first half hour; we are getting towards Parapan, and clearing the outskirts of Giurgevo. Night has overtaken us, and under cover of its softness I am taking forty winks. I begin to think that after all it is not so bad. This reflection has time fully to lodge itself on my brain when I see my leaders (I always had four-in-hand) looking in at me, whilst the carriage stops with a jerk.

Knowing the horses had no business to be so inquisitive, I look out and see a Russian sentry offering the point of his bayonet to the nose of my near leader; this had brought him round, and closely pursued as he was by his tormentor, had placed us, correspondent, horses, carriage, and sentries, very much of a heap. I had to get out, walk about a mile, wait about an hour until an officer could be found, who took me to his general, who to catch a poor unhappy correspondent jumped out of his bed in his trousers, and then discovered it was I, and I discovered it was General Schmidt, the general in command around Giurgevo, opposite Rustchuk, and with whom I had dined some three days previously at Bucharest.

We took a long drink and had a cigar together,

and this done, I trudged back over my mile to my
carriage to endure the rest of the troubles that a
correspondent has to undergo, even in one short
night. At General Schmidt's request, I gave a
lift to a young officer, and, leaving the environs of
Giurgevo at about half-past ten of the evening of
a fine bright moonlight night, we came on the first
Russian outposts about half-past eleven, and from
then until our arrival the following morning at
Zimnitza, were vigilantly challenged about every
twenty minutes.

The road, if it can be so called, made up as it is
of ruts and holes, runs all the way to Brigadir
within two hundred yards of the river-bank, and
affords a full view of the river and Bulgarian line
of hills. Along this road the patrols kept a constant communication one with the other, so that
what had happened to the Turk at Turnu Magurelli
through his want of vigilance, could never have
happened by the same want to the Russian.

All night through we met large bodies of infantry moving slowly and silently in the direction of
Zimnitza, there to cross the river and form part of
the main or centre army now advancing towards
Tirnova ; solid, sturdy-looking fellows, begrimed

with dust, heavily loaded with packages, yet marching on with a cheerful look and a pleasant word for any one who addressed them. They marched irregularly, in loose open order, in seeming rather carelessly, but not in reality, as they kept all well within the position allotted to each company, and no stragglers or laggards were to be seen.

Arrived at Petrosani, about half-way to our destination, the young fellow with me, on reporting himself to the officer in command, was desired to remain, as his services were required for some special work or another; so that here we parted, after making a cup of tea by the help of burning paper and a pewter teapot, in the schoolhouse of the village where he had lodged some days previously, having taken possession of it in the following prompt and soldier-like manner: On his arrival, finding all the other houses occupied, he spied the schoolhouse, and opening its door, discovered some dozen of the youth of the village listening to a discourse from the master on the virtues of the Russian army and nation generally. Entering, he took him gently by the ear and led him politely to the door, the master bowing repeatedly under his hand. Since that moment the primary education in that village is at a discount, and my friend has a comfortable dwelling.

As I continued to near Zimnitza the heat and dust became almost unbearable, great clouds of the latter rushing across the plains bordering the river, entering eyes, nose, and ears, and causing real suffering both to one's self and the poor beasts drawing me. Nor were my discomforts ended on arrival at Zimnitza—a dusty, dirty, straggling village, perched on a sloping plain, through which runs the Danube, and commanding a magnificent view, both up and down, of that glorious river.

Two days after I was back in my old quarters at Poradim, which during my absence, I learnt, had been menaced by the Turks, they having made an attack on our left. Swarming out like bees over the vine-clad hills to the right of the position at Radisevo and in between our own lines of Sgalinça and Pelisat, they had succeeded early in the morning of the 31st of August in surprising our pickets, capturing one of our advanced redoubts, and occupying the high ground dominating the level plain (planted with Indian-corn and vines) which runs back from the Plevna front to the head-quarters of Poradim and Karagac.

The fighting I learnt had been very severe, since, even in the first hour of the battle, one of the Russian redoubts had been taken by the Turks, re-taken by the Russians, and again re-taken by the Turks. At about eleven o'clock the Russian infantry fire rolled out strongly, and checked for a short while the Turkish advance.

General Zotow having appeared on the ground with a division of reserves, made at the Turks on the hill-crest, who began to drop rapidly. I do not know whether the Turks originally intended to attack our left or not, or whether they were forced to change the direction of the attack, but the advance veered to the left and rushed at the Russian trenches with a shout. Though met by a storm of balls from the Russians, they charged repeatedly for some fifteen minutes, then having had enough for the moment began to withdraw, carrying off their wounded.

However, soon afterwards they re-formed and went at the Russian trenches once more, dashing themselves at and falling within a few yards of the mouths of the Russian rifles, covering with their dead the slope on the crest of which were dug the Russian lines; the attack was terrible, but the

Turks were again repulsed, and again they retreated up the hill. Their third attack was
sheer madness, as it was evident they had made
no impression whatever on the Russian line of
fire, which kept up steadily its continual roll of
firing, and was strongly supported by well-posted
reserves. They were therefore easily repulsed once
more, and fearful loss was the result to them of
their hardy attempt; they fell back slowly, gathering
up their wounded and dead as they went, though
pursued by a murderous fire from the Russian right,
left, and centre, abandoning the redoubt they had
captured in the morning and retreating into their
own lines, to which they were pursued by our
cavalry, who made many prisoners.

It is difficult to understand the reasons for this
attack, unless Osman Pacha, tired of waiting, wished
to feel his enemy and try and ascertain by drawing
their forces what his enemy's dispositions were.
Osman gave proof of considerable ability in his
mode of attack, as it was made so suddenly and
with such violence as to take by surprise the leading Russian redoubt, and hurl back for the time
a portion of our centre; unfortunately, or rather
fortunately for the Russians, the Turks did not

appear to care about obtaining any decided results, as they attacked with too few men to enable them to profit by what they had gained. Their loss was considerably over 2,000 ; a serious loss to an army defending such extensive lines as those of **Plevna**, and cut off as the Turks were from reinforcements.

I have not as yet said anything of the Roumanian army, but as it played a considerable and very honourable part in the battle known as the third attack of Plevna, it certainly deserves mention. Its composition and organisation had been the object of much care and study on the part of Prince Charles ever since his election to the Principality, and he had succeeded in forming an army, or rather a large corps, of some 40,000 men well equipped and sufficiently well drilled. He naturally therefore, after the manner of all small princes on their promotion, wished to see how soon he could melt it down in an active campaign, and try for himself the noble sport of kings.

The Roumanian country was dead against his taking any active part in the war; but when the Czar, after the second reverses of Plevna, sent him an urgent appeal, calling him "My dear brother," and asking his help, he, in spite of the warning and

protests of all parties, ordered General Manu with
5,000 men to cross the river and occupy Nicopolis.
Manu did this, but being ordered by General
Krudener to advance beyond that town, refused;
his refusal was complained of by the Emperor, and
Prince Carl took away his command, transferring
it to General Angelesco.   The Roumanians constructed a bridge for themselves at Corabia, a place
thirty kilometres to the west of Nicopolis, and
hesitated some time as to whether they should
advance or not farther into Bulgaria.   However,
on Prince Carl being made Generalissimo of the
allied armies, they were moved into position on the
extreme right, and, constructing batteries, were able
to be of the greatest service to the Russians, and
helped greatly towards the only success obtained on
the great fight of the 11th September, viz., the
capture of the Gravitza redoubt.

The men of this little army made right good
soldiers, but the officers were the veriest lot of
little "play at pipeclay" warriors anywhere to be
met with.   Their camp was continually filled with
new relays of their lady visitors; the subaltern
officers objected to marching, and generally rode
behind their troops in bullock-wagons or mounted

on horses requisitioned from their own or the Bulgarian farmers. I confess that when I heard that the Roumanian army was actually quartered on the Vid, occupying a position which I fully expected Osman Pacha would hourly attack, seeing that it was easily attackable, and Osman was known to have a considerable feeling of contempt, for Roumanian warriors, I felt confident that the Roumanian army would in all probability very soon be flying back over the Danube faster than it had come across. However, Osman did not attack; or if he intended doing so, which I think not improbable in his sortie on the 31st of August, he missed their position, as they were never at any moment molested, Osman contenting himself once with a small demonstration against them by his Egyptian troops on his left.

On the 3rd of September Skobeloff added to his rising fame by the capture of the extremely important position and town of Loveca (Lovatz).

Going afterwards towards Loveca, which is a town situated on the river Osma, half way between Plevna and the Trojan Pass, I could not but remark that its great strategic importance ought to have early pointed out to the Russian commanders the absolute necessity of their occupying it ; but through the culpable ignorance of Levitski, no orders were given until after Osman had fully intrenched himself there; then a demonstration by Skobeloff in the early part of August was attempted, which merely resulted in a considerable number of good fighting men being transferred to the majority.

Skobeloff had been feeling the enemy in and about Loveca for some time, and together with the Prince Mirski at Selvi, had had several important skirmishes; the latter Prince had, as I have already told, been relieved from command by the Emperor, and his place taken by General Prince Immeretinski.

Leaving Selvi on the morning of the 2nd, Skobeloff (as an unattached general staff officer) took supreme command of the 2nd division (Immeretinski's), a rifle brigade which had just returned from the Shipka after a forced march in two days and a half of some sixty-five miles, a brigade of the 3rd division, and his own brigade of Cossacks. Arriving from Kakriva, Skobeloff first came on the enemy near Prisyaka, a position north-east of Plevna, and the Turks, after a short resistance, fell back on the fortified range of heights behind the town, and there awaited the attack. Skobeloff had placed his batteries over-night to the south of Loveca, in a position enfilading the heights held by the Turks; at Slatina he had placed his Cossacks and a portion of his rifle brigade, so that as the morning broke bright and clear, it found him ready to begin the attack from a highly advantageous position, and should the day prove (as it did) successful, his cavalry were in a position to prevent the Turks falling back and adding their numbers to the strength of the garrison at Plevna.

It was a glorious and impressive sight, on the morning of the 3rd, to watch the gradually advancing lines of glistening bayonets crowned by patches of silver-grey smoke shining through the trees, and marking the advance of the attacking force, while the echoes from the mountains gave back (gaining each moment in strength and rapidity) the sharp bark from the guns of the Russian field-batteries. The Turks fought as usual uncommonly well, and as we outnumbered them three to one, they being about 7000 to our 21,000, it is astonishing they stood against the overwhelming numbers of our battalions. The roll of the musketry coming up to the summit of the hill (on which we were posted watching the battle) in one continuous rattle, mingling with the never-ending whirr of the shell, made a babel of sounds impossible to describe. So long were we in making any impression on the enemy, that Skobeloff feared for a time his attack had failed, and it was only by the ceasing of the fire from the Turkish batteries that he was induced to continue the attack and win the town so necessary to the success of the contemplated assault on Plevna. Such as were left of the Turks made their way out due west, pursued by the Russian cavalry; the difficult nature of the ground aided them, and they were able to make good their retreat.

On September the 5th I called on General Krudener at Karagac, in company with Mr. Boyle of the *Standard* and another correspondent. I went to ascertain the meaning of certain "great-gun" sounds which had come wafted down to my quarters from the direction where the Roumanians were posted, and which had given rise to the most alarming reports. I found the old General in a terrible state of agitation. He was perusing at the time an account of his defeat at Plevna as given by Mr. Forbes, and he was far from complimentary in his comments on the truthfulness of that gentleman's narrative. He did not seem to mind the account so much as he did what he considered the presumption of an ignorant civilian (as he considered Mr. Forbes) in commenting upon him, an old long-tried and previously very successful soldier, insisting that Mr. Forbes' letters contained only superficial remarks such as could never be made by a military man who had played the game of war, but only by one who, confident in the mistaken proverb " that onlookers always see most of the game," indulged in vituperative abuse, applying the words " dotards," etc., to men whose only fault was to have become white-headed in gaining experience.

He was very severe indeed upon the " Major Archibald," and when, in an unlucky moment for himself, MacGahan dropped in, in the middle of the conversation, and with a smile (anticipating naturally, as a representative of the Russian organ, an assured welcome) announced himself as the *Daily News,* and consequently a colleague of the offender, the old man's wrath fairly broke out, and he said some few pointed words to Mr. MacGahan for repetition to his colleague.

This is how " the batch of correspondents," as Mr. Forbes describes them, appeared before General Krudener, and were not, as Mr. Forbes says,

10

summoned by that General to listen to his defence, and take up arms for him against his doughty assailant, the distinguished correspondent of the *Daily News.* Consequently, perhaps the old General did not deserve to be shot, as Mr. Forbes so strongly opined he did, for contravention of military law in defending himself against a one-sided attack.

The preparations for the third and, as it was at that time supposed, the final attack on Plevna, had been going on for some time. General Zotow, who, as chief of the staff to Prince Charles of Roumania, had virtually the ordering of everything connected with it, had taken some little trouble, although I cannot say that he had taken very much, in seeing that the plans proposed by the head-quarter staff should be fairly carried out. He had also caused rifle-pits and intrenchments and stands for batteries to be erected on all the favourable and commanding sites between Plevna and his rear on the Osma river, over which he had begun to construct a further bridge, so that had we been obliged to retreat, we might, had these rifle-pits been occupied, perhaps have annoyed the enemy in his advance, and we might have been able to have got over that bridge had it been finished, but not being so, our preparations for the great attack were not complete.

For some two days previous to the Friday morning of the 7th, the day on which the ball was about again to be opened, there was a something in the air denoting a great movement of masses round and about us, yet there was little to be seen; a good deal of talk amongst correspondents, making them correspondingly thirsty and causing a good many "dead marines" to be found in and about their quarters, plenty of whispering amongst junior aides-de-camp and other small fry of imperial, head-quarter, and general staffs, stray waifs of rumbling sounds, brought by the softly blowing breezes stirring the scorched grass on the surrounding plains, as heavy artillery drawn by fourteen yoke of oxen to a gun was dragged wearily to the front, or caused by brigades of cavalry moving to occupy positions to the extreme left, in order to cut off the retreat of an army which we all confidently believed must this time at least make way in Plevna for our Muscovite men; the generals not only firmly believed but were so assured of this, that their great and mistaken anxiety was, not about their getting into Plevna, but the route Osman would take in his

10—2

attempt to get out. It is inconceivable (and only
demonstrates what tyros at war Turkish generals
were coping with), yet is a fact, that although it was
known that the whole of the rear was open to the
retreat of the Turkish forces, should they be forced
to evacuate Plevna, yet that a "Sedan" was
confidently expected, and the word was on every
one's tongue.

Except for the purpose of making plain my narrative of what I saw and was engaged in of the attack
on Plevna, it is almost needless to write of the
country around Plevna, or of the plan of the third
attack (such as it was) on that much-suffering town,
so often have both subjects been already written of.
I will therefore give but a very short account of all
that took place on the one or two days of the 5th
and 6th of September, and then begin in the next
chapter my experiences of the four great days of
battle which ended so disastrously to the Russian
arms.

Prince Charles of Roumania, promoted to the
chiefdom of Russia's principal army allied to his
own, had in round numbers under his control some
74,000 men, who were quite equal in courage
and ability to the task of taking Plevna by a

coup de main, or in almost any other way, had their chiefs not frittered away their strength, spoilt their courage, and wasted through contemptible ignorance the advantages at their command. Prince Charles of Roumania found himself also at the head of some 400 guns, twenty of which were great field-pieces, known in Russia as twenty-four's, and had been drawn at an expenditure of great labour to a position almost within the Turkish lines, these were under the able direction of Colonel Exten, already justly celebrated for the batteries he had so ably constructed opposite Rutschuk.

It was dusk on the evening of the sixth, when I met these great-guns toiling over the vast sweeping plains and through the fields of corn towards the hill chosen for the site of the battery they were to form ; and I rode for a short time with the Colonel. He expressed his fears that he would hardly get up before daybreak, so slowly moved the fourteen pair of oxen drawing them ; he also told me that in the darkness of such a night it would be very difficult to hit the ridge topping the valley which he had already selected ; however I knew my man, and knew that whatever he had planned to do, he would do it, and so it proved. The next morning at break of day I found him where he was expected to have been, but of that in my description of to-morrow.

As I rode back towards my quarters, from the direction of Bogot in which I had been, I met bodies of troops in all directions advancing that way. Detachments of the 9th and of the 4th corps were slowly wending their way to occupy the positions assigned them for the momentous event of the morrow ; columns of cavalry with dancing pennons, regiments in line sweeping forward, the light from the fires of the poor Bulgarian refugee camps flashing on their bayonets, silently and steadily plodding onwards, each soldier of them going as quietly to possible death and more than probable wounds and suffering as though he were returning to his village home after a day's ploughing or peasants' work ; ambulance trains, and trains of wagons carrying the soldiers' knapsacks and provisions, creaking and groaning as they crept forward.

The arrangements for the coming morrow were not of a very strategic kind, being summed up in the two words " brute force." Big and little guns were to hammer away at the enemy's positions and redoubts, and as soon as it was supposed that the enemy had been a little demoralised by their iron hail, Russian soldiers were to scramble over hill and dale, parapet, *chevaux de frise*, and ditch, and consummate the work begun by fine touches with the bayonet. The attacking lines were to be drawn from a position at Bivola on the Vid, the extreme Roumanian right by a cordon of batteries, more or less advanced, at the back of the village and on the heights of Gravitza through Radisevo towards Tuchevnitza, to the east of which, by Bogot to Loveca, General Immeretinski with the 2nd division, and Skobeloff with one brigade of the 4th, his Cossacks, and the rifles, were echeloned. A brigade lay also somewhat to the south of Loveca, in order to extend and circle round to the west should Osman Pacha be driven out and attempt to make his way towards the Trojan Pass. It will thus be seen that the dispositions of the troops formed a very extended segment of a circle, the weakest part of which was its centre, as was abundantly proved on the morning of the 11th.

The Roumanians were expected to divert the attention of the enemy, and by threatening them over the old ground take off their attention from the main attack. This was I believe the programme, but as there was in very truth no plan of *main attack*, the early provision was useless. What Levitski's idea was in his attack of the 11th, will always remain one of those things which " nobody knows," not even omitting the originator. He seemed to have begun with some sort of idea that his attack should be made over the ridges on the left centre, strengthened by an advance from the left upon the redoubts actually overhanging Plevna; then he lost himself, and his mind got into a fog as dense as was the fog on the actual day of the assault. Plevna itself was, by the natural formation of the ground around it, capable of being turned into an easily defended intrenched camp, presenting as it did different elevations, offering every advantage to a military eye seeking to profit by the experience gained in the two previous unsuccessful Russian assaults.

In addition to the well-chosen ground which Osman Pacha had so ably selected as the spot for protracting for some months the life of the doomed state of which he was one of the leaders, he did not forget the aid afforded him by the superiority of his weapons over those of his enemy, his Krupp guns and his Peabody-Martini being vastly superior to the Russian field-pieces and the Berdan rifle; added to which his boundless wealth in cartridges enabled him to pour upon the cleared ground lying between him and his enemy a ceaseless fire, both day and night. The town itself lay in a hollow protected by spurs of hills and a deep ravine, and the attempts made to take it by assault must be for ever regarded as a criminal disregard of the proper care which all chiefs of armies should have for the lives of their men, and should further be accepted as a warning by nations not to undertake war in a cheap way. The true motive of Krudener's assault of the 31st July is to be found in the pecuniary difficulties of Russia. To the fear of a protracted campaign, and that August might pass, and its passage bring rains in September, the lives of men were as nothing. Her leaders knew (as is proved) that they had plenty of men to bring out, but they did not wish, on account of the expense, if it was possible to avoid doing so, to bring them. All Russia wanted at that time was a few striking successes in Bulgaria, sufficient to bring the Imperial hero of Tsarke-Seloë on a level with the all-conquering hero of the Lorraine-Alsatian provinces, and further to get into their hands

the fortresses of the Quadrilateral by inducing the
English ministry to put a pressure on the Porte
(relying on the supposed fear England felt of seeing
Russian troops in Roumelia), and get it to accept
terms of peace. Of course as matters have turned
out, this would have been better and more advantageous to both England and the Turk than the
present " pig in a poke " relations of all parties, but
nations are, as individuals are, often strongheaded.

CHAPTER VIII.

THE morning of the 7th September was bright and clear, with a strong wind tempering the great heat of the almost tropical sun, and clearing away the smoke from the guns of the great battery of twenty 6-inch guns, which, at half-past six that morning, had opened a sudden fire on the intrenched camps of the Turks.

By working steadily and silently all the previous night, Colonel Exten had succeeded in establishing one large battery of twelve guns on a small plateau immediately facing the great Gravitza redoubt; and again, below this plateau, and to its right, another battery on the edge of a hill rather nearer to the enemy; to the right of them, again,

were the field-batteries belonging to General
Krudener's corps; and again, to their right, and
somewhat in rear of the Gravitza village and redoubt,
were the Roumanian batteries. To the left of the
twelve-gun battery were posted, amidst low trees
and brushwood, on the ridge running towards
Radisevo, the guns of the 16th division. In all,
some 300 field-pieces were facing the number-
less Turkish works guarding the approaches to
Plevna.

Putting up a good lunch in my light four-horsed
barouche, and tying my saddle-horse behind, I trotted
off, in company with Mr. Boyle of the *Standard*,
over the plain, up and down the strongly accentuated
hills, through the village of Sgalinça, and up on to
the plain through which runs the main *chaussée* of
Plevna to Bulgareni and Sistova. When within
sight of the white puffs of smoke curling up over
the hills in my front, my friend and myself, leaving
the carriage under charge of my courier, mounted
and rode away along the *chaussée*. A short trot
brought us within easy view of the great redoubt
which Krudener had suffered so much from on the
30th July. It was slowly sending, from time to
time, its great Krupp shells, first at a Russian

battery, then at a Roumanian, taking very little notice of Exten's batteries which were keeping up a steady round fire on it. In all the hollows on either side of the *chaussée,* large bodies of Russian infantry were posted, lounging about, their arms stacked, and roasting at little camp-fires the "cocorousse," or small ears of Indian corn.

Turning to my left, I rode along the brow of a hill which looked down the valley, and along the ravine across which our left-hand batteries were playing, and from that point could plainly make out the clusters of Turkish batteries parallel and in rear, evidently well-constructed, but rather too open, little trouble being taken to hide the exact position of their guns. Besides these redoubts, trenches and rifle-pits scarred the sides of the hills in all directions.

On one hill I found General Krudener, sitting watching the play of the guns all round him—from his own batteries, from Colonel Exten's great-gun batteries, from the two hundred and odd guns to the right and left of him—and listening to the angry whirr of many tons of iron hurtling through the air, and raising, as shell after shell burst on the open ground, or on the parapet of a redoubt, clouds of yellow dust. The enemy had between eighty and ninety guns firing on us.

Wending my way along in rear of the batteries, I came to the great twelve-gun battery, and there had tea with Colonel Exten, remaining with him for some time, looking along his guns as he fired them, and watching the admirable precision with which shell after shell ploughed its way through the great banks of mud and sand forming the parapets of the opposing Turkish redoubts.

I then wandered on and over the hills in the direction of Radisevo ; but hearing that this village was still in the hands of the Turks, I halted and contented myself with watching the firing, and noting how little damage was done. Of four batteries which I visited, casualties were reported *nil*, the fifth had had one gunner wounded in the foot, and this though some one thousand shells had fallen in and around them. Later on in the day, I moved round by Tucenica, and joined Skobeloff in a ride along the Loveca-Plevna positions. We found out, however, but little. A few shells were fired at us as we ascended the slopes commanded by the Turkish guns on the S.E. ridge above Plevna. Everywhere along the crest of the hills masses of Russian infantry lay hidden among the vines, and the artillery horses of the different batteries were picketed along in their rear. The ground was torn up along this whole seven-mile line, and fragments of iron lay about in every direction.

Friday wore away, nothing of any moment occurring, the enemy replying vigorously from the larger redoubts, and seeming to feel our fire on the outer line along the Radisevo valley. The only gain of any moment we could take to ourselves this day was that we had driven the Turks out of their intrenched camps, and forced their men to lie about in the hollows, in which they were visible to us with the aid of our glasses. Meeting Krudener, he said to me, "There will be nothing to-day;" so, at about five, I rejoined my carriage, and drove back to Poradim to write my letters.

The next morning, Saturday, September 8th, saw me once more on the hill with Krudener, who, thorough old soldier as he is, had spent the night roosting on his perch amid the corn, and under cover of its darkness had shifted his batteries some six hundred yards closer to the enemy. At daybreak, the whole of the Russo-Roumanian batteries had reopened their fire, to which the Turks in their turn

were lazily replying.   The damage done to the
Gravitza redoubt had been repaired, and the Turkish
positions seemed in nowise different after their nine
hours of severe battering by our guns.

On our right, the Roumanian batteries had
also advanced during the night, and had placed
themselves in a position to do really effective work
on the Gravitza redoubt, which seemed to be the
end and object of all their firing.

In the afternoon (much to the disgust of my
coachman) I moved my carriage up under the flag-
staff of the great battery, determining to camp there
until the results of this very slow battle should be
known.   At about three in the afternoon, standing
watching the effect of our firing, and cursing the
monotony of our apparently fruitless efforts, a great
blaze on our left sprang up, and I could see Turks
jumping over their glacis and running for their lives.
A shell had found its way into the magazines of one
of the redoubts.   A long, low, rumbling sound, and
another sheet of flame, and one of the Turkish
redoubts had disappeared.

The Turks must have lost a good many men by
this accident.   For a few moments after this the
firing ceased completely, until it was noticed that the

Turks in the Gravitza redoubt were calmly with-
drawing a couple of their great-guns, to which
they had harnessed fourteen bullocks each, and were
quietly stealing off with them under our very noses.
Every battery within range opened fire, yet not
one shot struck. The ground was ploughed up
over them, in front, behind, on both sides; shells
burst in the air, but the bullocks pensively and successfully carried away the guns, and our gunners
looked blank with vexation. These two little inci-
dents occurred about half-past four, and I was about
to give up for the second day, as for the first, anything further happening than the interchange of
shot and shell between Russ and Turk, when suddenly a heavy musketry firing to our left caused
slumbering officers, vagrant Cossacks, and disappointed correspondents to wake to the lively thought
that something was about to change the uneventful
sameness of the last thirty-six hours' bombardment.

As I looked over the sunlit valley to my left,
standing on the summit of the hill, I could see
(away beyond the bend below me made by the
lower ridge hiding Radisevo) a dense blue and white
smoke rising from two directions at the same
moment. Away to the right a creeping cloud,

11

closing in on the Loveca road, showed that the
Turks were out of their intrenchments, and the
thickness of the cloud, always receding, that the
firing was actually advancing. What was it? Was
it a sortie of the garrison to turn our left, or was it
a retreat of the whole garrison of Plevna along the
Sophia road? Neither. It was Skobeloff—*toujours*
Skobeloff.

He had been poking his dragoons along the hills
running parallel with the Loveca road, and they,
pushing too far, had come on the redoubts with
which the Turks were endeavouring to cover the
only road open to their retreat, should such become
necessary. The Turks had sallied forth and driven
in the dragoons. Skobeloff seized the moment (as
he very naturally would) to punish them; and, advancing with a portion of the second division,
attempted to bring on a serious attack. The Turkish
right warmed to the occasion, and, filing out of
the redoubts, took up positions some few hundred
yards in their front, occupying the upward slope of
the wood-crowned hills separating the lines of the
two opposing armies.

As I rode from the right to the left, there was
one thing puzzling to me—namely, that the fire,

instead of closing in on me, was receding, and for some time I was loath to understand what it was (so interested does even an impartial man become in the side he is with); but the fact was too plain not to become soon apparent. The Turks were driving our men up the hill and back away in the direction of Prestova. And the enemy, like the badly-led set they were, did not know the success they were gaining, and that they were actually in between our centre and our left—that is, between the left of Zotow's corps and the right of Skobeloff's and Immeretinski's command. Of this I had abundant proof, as I shall shortly show.

As the fire receded I rode on; first down the road leading (in continuation) from the left batteries stationed below the 16th division, up over the crest of the hills commanding the valley by Radisevo, then, creeping out to a long spur of a hill covered with vineyards, found myself in the middle of a pretty thick artillery fire, and on a field strewn with dead and dying horses. This was the edge of the corner of the Turkish advance, and the left of the 16th division. Here the rattle of the rifles was again very plainly heard; and at this point my misfortunes began—misfortunes mingled with good chances, and lasting until the following morning, close on daybreak.

First, then, riding along the edge of the hill, a splinter of shell, coming from some invisible whole, struck my stirrup-iron, breaking the outer part, passed underneath my horse's belly, making an inch furrow in the ground some four feet beyond. The weight of my body occasioned by the wrench separated the remaining part of the iron, leaving me without a rest for my right foot. (I mention this accident, as it was a source of considerable anxiety to me farther on in the night.) I dismounted, and tried to lengthen the stirrup-leather, to accommodate matters; but finding it too short, remounted and continued with one stirrup only.

Riding as I was from Radisevo, and arriving a little towards the south-west, I felt sure I must be close on the Loveca-Plevna road, but felt no anxiety, as in front of me, hidden away in the vines and cornbrakes, and lying under the shelter of the hills, were men of every arm of the Russian service.

As I continued, I could not help noticing that these lines of men were becoming thinner; and at last I came to a spot where, the shells obliging me

to gallop over an open for full half a mile, I could
see for the moment no Russians whatever. I drew
rein, thinking that perhaps I was doing quite
enough for my papers. And as I sat and thought,
out jumped from behind a bush a Russian advanced
picket, his rifle full-cock at his hip, and his eyes
showing me that it was his full intention to know
all about me, or " double his first finger."

I called out " Russki !" tried him in English,
French, German, and even a little bad Italian. He
kept in the same awkward position, advancing as he
beckoned sideways with his head, to make me understand I was to dismount. I did not hesitate ; I
did as I was bid. And then began a jumbled
wrangle between us—I trying to ask for an "officern
Russki," pulling out of my satchel paper after paper
and pass after pass, stamped with the Russian arms,
and he trying to impress on me that I was his
prisoner—a fair captive of pure Turkish lineage.
Fortunately for me, being an outlying picket, he
could not leave until the guard came round. So after
about an hour (one of the most unpleasant, I think,
I ever recollect spending), a sergeant came up to see
if all was right, and, as he knew how to read, looked
over my papers and the badge on my arm, compared

my number with that on General Stein's certificate, and told the sentry to let go my horse's head, which he did as quietly as though nothing had happened, and as if he had not kept me under a nasty shell-fire from the enemy for close on an hour.

Considerably ruffled, I gave up my pursuit of Skobeloff, and turning my back to the rapidly-setting sun, galloped off in the direction which, I supposed, would soon carry me back to the spot where my servant, waiting with my carriage, would have a good supper ready for me—my mind especially dwelling on a certain tin of *paté de foie gras* which I knew was in possession of my friend Boyle, whose wagon was encamped close by me. Fate had, however, ordered otherwise. As I rode down the valley, on the left-hand ridge of which was stationed the 16th division, and into which the Turkish shells were every moment plunging, I turned up a bridle-path, which should have brought me out on to the batteries above. Riding I came on two officers sitting side by side on the slope ; one was Kriloff, commanding the 4th corps (Zotow's—Zotow acting as chief of the staff of the besieging army of Plevna), the other Colonel Tickenmanyeff, chief of staff of the 16th division.

The latter beckoned me as I rode past, noticing the direction I was coming from and seeing my *brassard*, and cried : " Who are you ?"

Riding up, I answered : " Correspondant du *Goloss*."

" Oh ! doesn't Skobeloff want reinforcements ?" and he closed his left eye as he spoke.

" Les Généraux Russes ont ordinairement toujours besoin," I answered.

He said a heap of eager words in Russian—which I, not knowing that language, could not understand —to his companion, General Kriloff ; evidently persuaded the latter, against his better judgment, to write a something on a small piece of paper ; then, jumping to his feet, was over the path and on the crest of the hill with the agility of a newly-appointed lamplighter. I heard his voice, shrill and clear ; I heard a hum of voices, a merry sort of subdued whisper, as some 2000 men, lining the edge of the summit of the hill, whither I had followed my Colonel, rose to the few words uttered. I saw him turning in the direction from which I had just come, and I said, " May I come with you ?" He nodded an assent ; and from that time until the following morning at half-past six, I never lost sight of him ;

and I am glad I did not, or my life would have
been of little value.

The darkness was growing as, closely following
the lead given by the Colonel, we plunged down the
side of the ravine (for hill it cannot be called, so
steep was it) in the direction given by two Cossacks
taking the lead, and whom, in the faint light, I
thought I could recognise as having already met
with when with Skobeloff at Selvi.

As I rode I felt my spirits rising, notwithstanding my hunger and fatigue, when I looked up and
saw swarming down towards me, with that peculiar
hum of " men on march," two whole battalions of
well-armed, plucky soldiers; and I thought this is
the way we correspondents should ride—none of
our solitary poking about desolate fields on still
more desolate nights, but with a full 2000 behind
us, with a colonel of staff alongside, and a colonel-
commandant following.

And so on we went, our horses snatching a drink
as they crossed the different fords, and the men
drinking as they waded through the rivulets, their
rifles and pouches held above their heads, and some
of them often to their breast in the water. On we
went, stumbling over stones, riding on the sides of

flint-clad hills, jumping and pressing our poor, tired beasts over little running streams, or scrambling, as best we could make them scramble, through ruts and deep-cut fissures, followed always by the tramp of the 2000 at our back. Twice I was down, but without hurt, before we got into a long and large valley, and the Colonel, Tickenmanyeff, halted to look about him, pull his men together, and—will you believe it?—find out where he was!

We halted; I took out my case, lit a cigar, and offered him one. Then said he to me: "Do you know where we are?"

"No, Colonel," said I; "don't you?"

"Pas du tout," was the nonchalant answer.

He then explained to me that feeling sure Skobeloff would be again attacked that night or the next morning (and so he was), he wished to be in the row, and for this had persuaded Kriloff to give him a couple of battalions, and allow him to seek Skobeloff's whereabouts. He understood that Skobeloff had crossed the Loveca main road, but was not sure.

"Then," said I, "Colonel, if that is the case, we are a great deal too much to our right."

He agreed with me, yet never thought of consulting with the commanders of the battalions (who, as I happened to know, knew something of the country). Such a proceeding would have been derogatory to a Russian staff officer.

I am not saying this to blame Tickemmanyeff, as all of his school would have committed the same error, and he himself is as brave and as clever a fellow as ever wore the cross of St. George; but I blame his school, which was of the school of the staff of Russia, and to which the lives of their men are as nothing to their own individual advancement.

After a halt of a few minutes, and as our men were formed in loose line behind us, we pushed forward again, Tickemmanyeff insisting on the strictest silence. And well he might, for he knew he was somewhat out of his reckoning, and that he was deep down in a valley almost impossible to get out of, steep rising rocks being on either side, enabling a few hundred men on its heights to destroy every life under his command without possibility of his retaliating even with any effect, setting aside any chance of escape. Yet he pushed on, taking them, as will be seen, straight to their doom, my cigar burning brightly in his mouth, and strict silence imposed on his followers. Why, our two Habanas showed a mile off.

Well, about an hour's march through this defile— steep banks growing every moment apparently steeper—began to weary the Colonel, so after a few moments of hesitation he turned to his left, and on getting to the almost perpendicular walls then hemming us in, put his horse at them, and leaning on the poor beast's neck, began an ascent which I following, never wish to see tried by any horse again.

Half-way up, the Commandant, a short, thick man, on a long-legged brute, tried to dismount, slipped his horse's legs from under him, and down they went together, sliding and gliding, kicking and crashing, into the darkness beyond. I left all to my beast, and how he did kick and pant and heave under me, standing on corners and ledges and jutting-out trees, and straining his neck and slipping, pulling himself together again, until at last, breathless and panting, he stood on the height of the great cliff.

He had climbed and was now on a plain on which the moon was shining placidly, in apparent cool contemptuous mockery of the efforts of the poor devils

to whom she was giving light, and by her light a
fresh danger.

As I came up to Tickenmanyeff, resting his horse
and waiting until the men should get up, there rang
out on the night air the clear shrill " Tra, la, la !" of
the Turkish alarm.

" Les Turcs," said I, and we whispered.   It is
strange how most men whisper when in a crisis in-
volving life.

" Non, non," said he.

But it was not " non, non."   For scarcely was
the negative out of his mouth when buzz, whirr,
buzz came the bullets about our ears.

Now behind us were swarming in a long extended line to our right and left the men we were
h eading, and as they gained the plain, without
troubling themselves about orders or about us, they
flung themselves on their bellies, and opened an
answering fire on the Turks.

Tickenmanyeff and I were within ten yards
of our own men, who were loading and firing as
rapidly as possible under, over, and round or
through, for aught they knew or cared, our heads,
and the bullets of the enemy were spinning past
us ; my beast was standing on its hind-legs, making

desperate attempts to break away out from the flashes of our own rifles burning right under his eyes, and all my energies were devoted to keeping Tickenmanyeff's black horse in sight, and sticking to my saddle, minus, as I have already said, one stirrup-iron.

The Colonel was doing all he knew to jump his horse through his men to their rear, and shouting with all his might, "A illuevo, a illuevo!" ("To the left, to the left!"); a cry which I myself took up, hoping it meant cease firing.

Then there was a lull, the Turks ceased firing, two or three shots were fired on our side, and all was still. My beast took the bit in his mouth, and galloped for some hundred yards straight towards the enemy. As I checked him and got him round I heard the stifled groans of a man beside me, and saw the outline of a half-sitting figure glaring at me from the ground some three paces off. As we were not close enough to the Turks, or they to us, to have had wounded of either side so near our line, it must have been some poor neglected devil of a Turk lying there, after the evening's fight, unable to crawl within his own lines, and forgotten by his comrades.

I got back, and found Tickenmanyeff in rear of our men, who were massing four deep just below the ridge of the hill we had a few minutes before so arduously climbed. There was a consultation; a man in the ranks was smoking a pipe; Tickenmanyeff struck it from his mouth. Then I heard the steady tramp of a line of men on the march on my right; two guns blazed at us, a roaring, crackling fire on our right flank lit up the ground, and showed us plainly a mass of advancing red fezzes. Our men answered with a faint cheer, fired a straggling volley, then for a moment I saw them like dissolving spirits in a pantomime vanishing with lightning rapidity into the gloom, down the hill they had just come up.

I caught sight of Tickenmanyeff bolting as hard as his horse could pelt along the plain and on the edge of the hill to the left, and I dug my spurs into my beast and flew after him, the bullets whizzing, and the flashes glaring in a semicircle behind me. My horse, mad with fear, required but little urging, and I was soon alongside the Colonel, who, as soon as he got out of the fire, pulled his beast into an easy gallop.

After riding on for a quarter of an hour or so

he dismounted and tried to force his horse down the steep sides of the cliff to get to •the valley we had come from; but it was no use, the beast, with a very proper sagacity, declining to make a step downwards. We then, taking our horses by the bridles, began scrambling along the edge, fearful of continuing along the summit as we could see the glimmer of the enemy's watch-fires about two or three hundred yards on the right.

Holding on to bushes, clinging by hands and knees to jutting pieces of rock, my bridle round my arm, and my poor brute struggling and slipping behind me, I toiled for two hours, my clothes torn and my hands covered with blood by thorn and bush. At last, coming out on to a corn-field, we again mounted, and I asked Tickenmanyeff,

" Where are we ?"

" Chut! ne parlez pas," said he, and I asked him no more questions.

In silence we rode at a foot-pace through corn-fields, up lanes, plunging over ditches, or stooping to clear overhanging boughs of trees. To our left great glaring flashes, followed by the heavy boom of the Krupp guns in the Turkish redoubt, showed us that we were a long way to the right of our proper road. Yet on through the still darkness, without any sign of hesitation, rode the Colonel, and I blessed my stars that that night developed in him a prodigious bump of locality, for about half after twelve we heard the rumble of wheels, and, coming on a telegraph-post, knew that we had struck the Plevna-Loveca *chaussée.*

My friend dismounted. I held his horse whilst he anxiously listened, marching away to his left. I lost sight of him in the gloom, then heard a challenge and his answer of " Officern Russki." I moved round, and came on a Russian picket. Providence had so befriended us as to cause our falling in between ours and the enemy's picket lines. A few hundred yards more to our right and we should have been either dead or prisoners.

From them we learnt that Skobeloff was at Brestovec. So, pushing across the *chaussée,* we moved on for that place, and overtook the General himself, coming in after an inspection of his lines. We rode up alongside, and Tickenmanyeff explained matters.

" Ah !" said the General, " then all the reinforcement you bring me is an English correspondent."

And turning to me, holding out his hand, said : " Stanley, I thank you for thinking of me."

We went to his quarters, a carpeted tent in a farmyard, and there drank in thankfulness to our prolongation of life, and supped upon borge-soup.

Skobeloff told me that he had attacked a redoubt, but had not succeeded in getting into it ; that his position at the moment was somewhat perilous, but that, if not attacked before morning, he would have so intrenched it as to make it impossible for the Turks to dislodge him.

Remounting our horses at two, the Colonel and I rode back through Tucenitza, passing, as we wen over the field of that day's fight, close by Brestovec, and through hordes of dogs sniffing and smelling at the stark, stiff dead, who lay dotting the ground, Russian and Turk together. War is a very horrid thing.

I lay down that night in the trenches above Radisevo, and slept for some few hours, covered over with a half share of the Colonel's cloak ; and we started to our feet at daybreak, suddenly awoke by a rapid roll of firing, and the bullets whizzing over us. The Turks made a demonstration of charging us ; but, being met by a fierce and well-directed fire,

12

moved back into their lines again.   It only lasted
for some twenty minutes; then, very tired and
hungry, I rode back in the direction of the great
battery, underneath which I had left my carriage,
and found, to my utter disgust, that my courier,
fearful of a stray shell falling his way, had taken it
back to Poradim.   I begged a breakfast of Colonel
Exten, then went off to tell General Krudener what
I had seen of Skobeloff.

Whilst talking to him, an officer rode in to say
that the Turks had reattacked that morning at daybreak, pouring out in great numbers from the two
redoubts at Krishing; but, as Skobeloff had told me
he would, he had strongly intrenched, and so was
able to repulse them (after two hours' hard fighting),
with considerable slaughter.

Sunday wore away, a lazy firing on both sides
alone breaking the stillness of its lovely afternoon,
and disturbing the quiet slumbers of the sixty or
seventy thousand men hidden away, and lying
sleeping, in and around the batteries under cover of
the vines and brushwood.

When in the big battery, Colonel Exten told me
he was about to move six of his guns to a position
some three miles farther west, so as to get them to

play well into the S.W. batteries defending Plevna.
He did so, and the guns so removed played a somewhat important part in the battle of the 11th, yet by
no means so important a one as they might, had
they been placed in a position farther to the left,
which would have enabled them to see the advance
of their infantry, and afford it support. But it was
not so, and was on a par with all the Levitski
management of these six days of battle. I have
not the presumption to criticise, further than by
drawing an inference of what was, and what might
have been, had the slightest attention been given by
the superiors to what their inferiors were about.
The whole seemed to me to be " happy go lucky."

The Emperor's birthday was approaching. Each
private of every regiment would on the Sunday
finish his three days' rations of biscuit, knowing
that when the 11th came something would be
attempted. But the *Almanach de Gotha* told Osman
Pacha the same story, and he was also preparing
a welcome. The Grand Duke and Nepochoichitski
had but one thought, like that which inspired
Sherman when he "guessed he'd send Savannah as
a birthday present to Abraham Lincoln," in the
execution of which Sherman was successful.

Levitski caught the thought, and such catching being rare with him, persuaded his august friend and protector, the Grand Duke Nicholas, to make an offering of Plevna to his Imperial brother. And yet Levitski must have known that he had but some 53,000 bayonets, if he had that, and I doubt it. He knew that his enemy was supposed to have upwards of 60,000, and occupied positions equal almost in strength to the lines of Sevastopol. And yet, in order " to do something," he sacrificed about 9000 lives.

Of course there is this to be said in his defence, that the feeling of the army gathered around Plevna was, that something should be done on the 11th of September, if it were only that it should die for the Czar.

It was resolved that the wishes of the army should be consulted, and though Levitski should have known that such an attack could scarcely succeed, yet he assented to its being undertaken. He had even, so I am credibly informed, predicted to the correspondent of the *Times* that another "Sedan" was to be witnessed, which interesting prophecy was duly telegraphed, received, and chronicled, and a most erudite article on the consequences to Europe of this event was inserted in the *Times*. Well, the event did not come off, as we all know; but what did come off, was another wonderful article, within a week of the first, announcing the contradiction of the prophecy, and calmly chanting, in the same assured breath, " I told you so."

Returning to Levitski and the general staff, or rather the staff actually in control of all the momentous movements of these two Russo-Roumanian armies before Plevna, I ask what can be said in their defence, when I am obliged to write that it took up its quarters in a village some fifteen miles and a half to the rear of its line of battle?

It is so easy to throw stones at men seated " on high places," that I have no wish to prove my aptitude. But I saw so much suffering, so many wounds, so great a quantity of dead, that I cannot help expressing my opinion that even grand dukes ought to have some muzzle put upon their readiness to order mere ordinary mortals to death and pain, unless they are willing also (in fair proportion) to expose their own well-cherished carcases to the same.

The subaltern princes of the Imperial family have

shown great pluck, the responsible princes of the
Imperial family have shone by the conspicuous absence of that quality, and their individual staffs,
with the exception of one or two of the aides-de-
camp generals of the Emperor (whom I have in my
mind), imitated closely their Imperial chiefs in this
absence.   On the 11th, I rode into the big battery
of six guns, which (well to the rear) was pitching
its shells on Plevna, and found at least half a dozen
aiguilleted heroes of the different staffs spying
through their glasses, their own lines a full mile
away from them, and they never thinking any more
than if they were witnessing a sham retreat at a
theatre, that perhaps it was their duty to be in
amongst them.

One fine, fat fellow turned to me as he shut his
glasses, and said :

"Allons, c'est tout fini ; venez prendre du tchaï."

It gives me pain to say these things of men who
have such qualities as have the higher class of
gentlemen of Russia.   I do not wish to be mis-
understood by any who may read so far, as to
pretend that the Russian officer has sunk into
this abject state of cowardice and unwillingness to
share in the active trials of the army which they

direct, but to show that it is not in the traditions of their army to do as other European officers.

It appears to them that a certain position bringing as it does with it a certain responsibility, also affords a certain immunity, and all I wish to point out is, that the Russian staff officer, as a class, takes far too often the shelter of this immunity.

CHAPTER IX.

THE THIRD ATTACK ON PLEVNA, FROM THE EVENING OF THE
NINTH TO THE NIGHT OF THE TWELFTH.

SUNDAY night and Monday passed without anything
of moment to relate; troops were gradually being
shifted from right to left, batteries were moved in
closer to the Turks, and General Krudener shifted
his quarters from the hill to the left of Gravitza to a
field overlooking Radisevo and in between that place
and Tucenica. It was evident that the morrow was
to be an eventful day; I rode round the positions
occupied by the 4th corps, and by the left of the
9th, and found everywhere a cheerful confident
courage in the soldiers and their officers, all ready to
sacrifice on the morrow their lives in order to present
their Emperor with the strongholds of Plevna.
Working-parties were busy bringing up piles of

scaling-ladders, and Engineer officers were creeping about dodging the sharpshooters of the enemy and selecting favourable places in readiness for the assault.

At half-past four, for the first time, the Grand Duke Nicholas rode round towards the left, but a shell kicking up the dust some two or three hundred yards from him, he retired to his quiet quarters at Radenica, half way to Bulgareno and about thirteen miles as the crow flies to the rear of his army.

Many different hours were fixed upon by the men as to the moment when the assault would take place, but it gradually leaked out that the battle was not to begin until one o'clock, and the grand assault to be at three. However, Russians propose, but in this case Turks disposed. Up to the evening of the 10th the weather had been most delightful, but towards sundown of that day it began to change, the sun setting grey and watery and the clouds threatening a bad day on the morrow. And so it proved; about three in the morning I awoke to find myself lying in a puddle, and a soft drizzling rain soaking me thoroughly.

At about eight I mounted, and riding for about an

hour towards the left, came upon Generals Zotow and Kriloff, who, with their respective staffs, had taken up a position in line with the reserves on a hill to the left of Radisevo and close behind Colonel Exten's newly-placed six-gun battery. In their encampment plenty, if not peace, reigned. The two staffs were fraternising together, and early in the day as it was, short nips of brandy and the contents of bottles of champagne were trickling down thirsty throats. The Generals sat in their carriages, the staff lay about on clothes spread on the ground, and we all merrily laughed and joked over the particular hotel we that night should patronise in Plevna; that our army was going to complete defeat and almost utter annihilation never for a moment entered the head of any one. Only once did doubt on the subject trouble us. Colonel Nevitski asked me how many men were, in my opinion, within Plevna. I answered, "Some 70,000," and asked in turn what was our attacking force? He replied, "About 38,000." Then noticing the blank look of wonder on my face, he laughed and said: "Oh no, we are about 80,000 strong." They were not though.

General Zotow sat at his little round table eating cold meat and game-pie, and his staff stood round distributing amongst themselves and to three hungry correspondents—Mr. MacGahan of the *Daily News*, Mr. Boyle of the *Standard*, and myself—the good provender provided, when we heard the crack of a rifle on our left, then a continuous roll like the steady beat of a drum.

"What is the matter?" said the General. "Why this is out of all rule; the Emperor himself fixed the hour of battle for one o'clock, and it is barely ten. It must be Skobeloff;" and Skobeloff of course it was. Whether he began it, or whether the Turks, fearful of being cut off to their right, endeavoured to feel our strength, I have not learnt; but as I rode away with Zotow to the front, I caught sight of a great streaming mass of Turks moving to our left by the Loveca road, and presently the firing extended from their right away up to our position opposite Radisevo. And such firing as it was! what to liken it to I know not, except to an endless roll of thunder. One would imagine that no line of men could possibly stand against it, and yet the patient steady Muscovite went on under it as calmly as possible. As I stood on the spur of a low hill, I watched the battalions forming into line, then marching out thin and scattered with a weak front line at first, and small columns of support fifty yards or more to their rear, then a longer line of reserve supports; but I also noticed that barely was the first line well under fire before its supports closed on it and it began to halt, then I saw the rear lines mingling with the supports so that all were together in line, or rather in open order, fighting as it were independently, with nothing in rear to support them, and the fierce fire of their enemy dropping them and thinning out their ranks. On went the line to within some 400 yards of the Turkish trenches; then little could be seen of it, except that to judge by the number of the wounded dragging themselves back it must be suffering greatly.

Every moment the firing grew hotter, and the line on which my glasses were fixed was, as far as I could make out, hidden as it was by the fog and smoke, hesitating as to what it could do. Kriloff noticed the position, and put in another regiment to support; but it was not a regiment, it was at least a division that was wanted. With the aid of this, my line (the one I was watching) struggled bravely up to the shelter-trenches of the Turks in front of the centre redoubts, then down the slopes, and from behind them came a fresh body of Turks marching

steadily on to the flank of the Russian advancing
line, and by its overwhelming fire forcing the three
regiments of the 4th corps to fall back towards
Skobeloff on the Loveca-Plevna road, leaving quite
a third of its number on the ground.   As the Turks
marched over the ground of the retreating Russians
they bayoneted the wounded.   Up the slopes of the
hill on which I stand a steady stream of ghastly
faces and blood-stained garments are carried or drag
themselves wearily and groaning towards their
ambulances ; and still the murderous roll goes on,
shells are hurtling and exploding all around.   In the
hollows in my rear are hid the reserves, now is the
time to put them in ; but no, it is not done ; the hour
fixed for the assault has not yet come.   Etiquette
said three o'clock ; but at one, half the work was
done, and had large bodies been hurried forward,
might have completed the success gained by Skobeloff
and Immeretinski on the left, who, being attacked
in the morning, had, by reserving their main fire,
induced the Turks to come out in the open, and
then poured it into them with deadly effect, driving
them up into their right-hand redoubts and covering
the Loveca valley with Turkish dead and wounded.

It was difficult to judge of the plan of the battle,

first on account of the length of the line, secondly because it was apparently being fought in detachments and without any great unity of action, and again on account of the denseness of the fog.

The original plan of the battle as given me by Colonel Novitski was simple enough : Skobeloff and Immeretinski were to open the fight by an attack on the redoubts in the bend of the Sophia road, the extreme Turkish right ; at the same moment the Roumanians were to attack from the south-east the great Gravitza redoubt, the extreme Turkish left, whilst General Kriloff in the centre stormed the lines in the immediate vicinity of Plevna.   The plan offered a fair chance of success had there been more men, and had the Turks not taken the initiative in the morning ; but the plan of battle became seriously damaged when the Turks, opening fire on Skobeloff the moment he began his march towards their redoubts on the right, attempted at the same time to take the offensive in their centre by storming the positions held by Kriloff on the ridge of Radisevo. In this they were not successful, being driven back with considerable loss, and had we then pushed forward all our reserves and made the attack general, it is not improbable we should have got into Plevna on that 11th day of September; but as I have said, it was not the hour fixed, so that our men were, when almost in the enemy's trenches, marched back, to be made again to march forward through the thick and tiring mud and over the bodies of their fallen comrades some hour or so later.

At about two Mr. MacGahan, Mr. Boyle, Mr. Jackson of the *New York Herald,* and myself, lunched off cold goose and Strasbourg pâté under a pretty smart shell-fire in the vines immediately by Kriloff's left centre; and I subsequently, in company with MacGahan, rode farther to our left to an excellent position commanding a good look up the valley and to the Gravitza redoubt to our right, and on to the redoubts which Skobeloff was hammering away at beyond the Loveca road on our left. The bullets and shell were flying about so thickly that we had to dismount, and tying our horses to the cornbrakes, creep along taking as much shelter as we could until we came to a halt under a tree and watched. Ah, that I could tell all I saw on that afternoon !

The day was a drizzling wet one ; to right and left and down the valley in front of me dense volumes of light smoke were slowly struggling up-

wards, whilst an indescribable babel of sounds filled
the air; from the Radisevo ridge above me on the
left over a hundred guns were flinging their deadly
missiles into the lines opposite them, and all
along from extreme right to left some 35,000
rifles were emptying themselves into the Turkish
trenches. As the fog was lifted by the wind, I could
just make out the forms of men wriggling through
vine and corn warily, and without firing, trying to
gain a position for a charge on the centre redoubt
near Plevna, and keeping my glasses fixed on them,
saw them huddling up together, then, jumping to
their feet, make a rush up the steep slope (in all
there were about ten battalions), and, scaling-
ladder in hand, make a dash at the parapets. A
lurid flame burst from these like the sulphuric
blaze of a great volcano, the whole ten battalions
disappeared enveloped in its smoke, then flame after
flame followed, lighting up with a fierce glow (so
rapid and continuous was the rifle-firing) the dense
dark smoke in which these ten devoted battalions
were struggling; the loss of life was appalling, not
one half the number got back, as with wild gestures
of affright they rushed downwards and backwards,
followed by the merciless bullets. Kriloff himself

dashed forward with part of a regiment to cover their retreat and try to lead them up again ; but the fire was too much, no mortal could stand against such pitiless pelting. It did make the attempt, the men wildly cheering as they rushed to the assault, but with the like failure.

I have already called attention to the astonishing fact, that during all this war the Russians steadily and zealously refused to learn by their disastrous experiences, that small bodies of men are not of use when employed against an intrenched enemy ; the rapid firing of the present day destroys so speedily and utterly any small body employed against it, that it is simply wasting life and means to attempt to cross a space exposed to a concentrated fire, unless the supports at hand are available to fill immediately the gaps which must of necessity be made in the first line of any advancing force.

Whilst I was watching the centre, the Roumanians on the right were giving proof of their metal by an attempt to take the great Gravitza redoubt. At about two they marched in from the direction of their own batteries on the heights, which were keeping up a steady and stinging fire on the great redoubt, and uniting with two battalions of

13

Krudener's command, filled the ditches, and by the aid of their scaling-ladders and evident pluck and determination, succeeded in effecting a lodgment, driving out the Turks at the point of the bayonet. This same redoubt had cost Krudener the lives of thousands of his command on the 30th, and it would have been supposed that any amount of troops would be ready to reinforce should the place once be taken; but no, not a bit of it. No troops were sent, notwithstanding the earnest appeals of the Roumanian and Russian officers in command of the attack, and the consequence was that at about five the Turks, returning to the attack, retook their redoubt at the point of the bayonet.

Hearing of this, Krudener himself rode over to the redoubt, and echeloning four Russian battalions and a Roumanian battalion of infantry, placed them under command of Colonel Schmelter, one of the Imperial aides-de-camp generals. These charging down from the covered ground immediately around the upper part of the village of Gravitza, flung them-selves into a sort of river ditch at the foot of a long open swell, a little above which stood the Gravitza redoubt. Major Kavidka, an aide-de-camp of Krudener's, unfurling the Russian flag, dashed up the ascent followed by all the men, who, with a wild cheer, flung themselves into the ditch surrounding it, and notwithstanding the fierce fire playing on them, placed their scaling-ladders against the parapet; as Kavidka led his men into the redoubt, a Turkish gunner, true to his work, was pulling the lanyard of his gun, and Kavidka with one sweep of his sword cut the hand from the wrist (I saw it myself lying on the ground when I went up to the redoubt on the following day) and shot the gunner through the head. Jumping then on the gun, he was waving on the men when a flying Turk turned and shot him through the breast. Colonel Schmelter, jumping in, was shot through the head, the bullet going through the forehead and coming out at the poll; yet with this fearful wound he contrived to live (though unconscious) for two days. As the Turks fled out, another battalion of Roumanians came up to join in the glory of this daring feat.

The same afternoon at four o'clock, Skobeloff, the undoubted genius of the hour, had advanced from the position Immeretinski had occupied on the Loveca-Plevna road to a position facing Krishine, the extreme right-hand Turkish redoubt. In the early part of the same day, Skobeloff had of his own initiative advanced twenty guns to within some 400 metres of the redoubt, and under cover of the fire of these guns, advanced to the attack.

When he considered the ground had been sufficiently prepared by artillery, he advanced a portion of the rifle brigade, which with the 2nd division, a brigade of the 9th, and his own irregular Cossacks, constituted the troops at his disposal, making in all 22,000 men. Forming his men into a semicircle, he made a rapid rush at the outlying works covering the great Krishine redoubt. There was a gentle slope leading up to this position, and before his men had half covered the ground between them and the enemy, they were met by such a withering fire from the Turks, that such of the front line as were not stricken down dead or wounded, fell back on the extended line supporting it, and that in turn had to retire and fall back on the reserve.

Skobeloff had remained to the right and a little in rear of the men, sitting on the caisson of an ammunition-wagon, when a shell dropped right into it, causing an explosion, blowing him up, killing fourteen of his staff, and scorching the hair of Kerow-pat-Kine his chief of the staff, but leaving Scobeloff, with the usual providential luck which he enjoyed throughout the war, perfectly safe and intact.

Finding he was not about to take the redoubt in the easy manner he had hoped, he mounted his white charger, dashed in amongst the men, and succeeded in rallying them. Rushing with the whole of his command up on to the outlying works, he carried them at the point of the bayonet, driving the Turks *pêle-mêle* into the great redoubt above them. His first object then was to fortify the position which he had taken, and he had barely succeeded in placing three guns inside, when the Turks, who had massed on their right under the belief that the main Russian attack would have come from that quarter, advanced and made an unsuccessful attempt to retake the works.

The fight was continued off and on the whole evening, and extending far into the night, Skobeloff being always able to hold his own, but sending repeatedly news of the success he had won to the rear, and begging for reinforcements, which were of absolute necessity to him, inasmuch as in the attack and subsequent defence the rifle brigade had been nearly "wiped out," and some 4000 of the 13,000 he had put into line were lying killed or wounded.

He held the position he had won all that night and
the next morning, the Turks making every effort to
dislodge him.   At 3.30 p.m., finding that it was vain
to hope for any aid from head-quarters, he determined to evacuate the works he was holding, and
as he carried out his intention, the Turks, moving
out *en masse*, drove him out of the position, back
to the one he held at Brestovec, capturing his
three guns and making upwards of 1800 prisoners,
and mowing down his men who, fighting to the last,
fell like corn before reapers.

As he gained his old lines at Brestovec, he met
an advancing column, which General Kriloff, acting
on his own responsibility, had sent to his relief.
It was, however, too late ; the day after the anni-
versary of the Czar proved equally as disastrous to
the Russian arms as the day itself.

Summarising the general results of the twenty-
four hours, commencing at ten o'clock on the
Tuesday morning, the 11th of September, it may be
said with perfect truth that neither side can claim
to have shown the faintest tincture of generalship.
The Turks had in the early morning of the 10th, as
I have already shown, made a severe irruption into
the Russian lines, and had succeeded in so bending

it in on the centre, that if they had continued their advance for another two hundred yards they would inevitably have taken the ridge of Radisevo. It is true that the Russians had in reserve the whole 30th division, but so extended was their line, at so many points was this reserve required, and so overwhelming was the force advanced by the Turks on one point in comparison with the opposition that could be offered at that point, that even at the very spot where the 30th division lay, they could have succeeded in cutting off the right of the Skobeloff-Immeretinski command from Zotoff's left, where the remaining divisions of the attacking army lay.

The only success of the day cannot in fairness be credited to the Russians; for though there were two Russian battalions and one Roumanian battalion which made the final attack on the Gravitza redoubt at 5.30 p.m., it must be borne in mind that the only effect produced upon that strong position by the constant cannonading of the three preceding days had been produced by Roumanian guns attacking it on its weakest point from the north-east and rear.

· On the following morning, Wednesday, Septem-

ber 12, I rode up to the positions occupied in the
early part of the fight by General Krudener, and
looking down into the great hollow before it and
the Gravitza redoubt, could make out a stream of
wounded dragging themselves painfully to the rear.
Riding in amongst them, I mounted to the village,
and from that on to the high ground forming the
crest above.

Thence I could see away to Plevna, its minarets
shining gaily in the morning sun, not having apparently suffered the slightest damage from the
mass of iron launched against it. Away on the
right I could make out the Russian and Roumanian flags over the frowning mass of earthworks
which had been so fatal to the soldiers of the
former nationality on the 30th of July. Riding
down into the advanced trenches, from which the
Russians and Roumanians had had to charge, I
came upon what were literally piles of dead bodies
and of wounded men lying in every posture which
agony had dictated, the living writhing and groaning in a pitiable condition of suffering, waiting for
the arrival of bearers to convey them to ambulances. Tying my horse to the wheels of an
ammunition-wagon, I crept up to the point where,

in the last attack, the Roumanians had formed up previously to charging into the battery.

Here shot and shell were still falling pretty thick, whistling bullets constantly bringing death into the ranks of the poor young Roumanian "Dorabensiti," who in their sheepskin bonnets, unaccustomed as they were to anything like war, had so gallantly vindicated their country from the suspicion that her men would prove to have as little character in the field as her women were supposed to have in the town.

I got into the redoubt that morning, and saw scenes which I never wish to witness again. The open part was then tolerably clear of both dead and wounded, who had been carried away or thrown over the parapets by the new occupants ; but in the galleries, where a desperate hand-to-hand fight had occurred, tortured humanity was to be seen in every form.

Riding back into the village of Gravitza itself, and hearing the crowing of cocks and the cackling of hens as lively as if no war was going on close by, I went into a small farmyard and saw two women sitting under the porch knitting calmly, and looking as comfortable as possible. There were strings of the red pepper-pods, which Bulgarian and Roumanian peasantry use so largely in cookery, festooned above their heads.

There, sure enough, I saw plenty of poultry, cocks strutting about in separate corners, each attended by a goodly following of hens. I had with me a young fellow I had picked up in Sistova, who was acting as my interpreter. By my directions he asked the women in very humble fashion if it were possible to have a chicken.

They replied in the negative, but one of them disappearing into the hut came back in a few seconds bringing with her two young turkey poults, which she sold me for tenpence. Showing that, so far from there being the desolation which had been so graphically described in the *Daily News* as following in the train of the Turkish troops, and in the *Daily Telegraph* as the immediate consequence of Russian occupation, the market-price for poultry in this village had not risen at all, though both Turks and Russians had been repeatedly passing through since the beginning of July.

The third attack on Plevna had come to an end, and there was nothing left for the commanders but to sit down again before the place and defend themselves against the constant charges and counter-charges which immediately began to explain the causes of the failure, and for the unfortunate soldiers and officers who had been hit to moan over the want of care and attention from which they were suffering.

Without for a moment pretending to say that the Russians were systematically careless of their wounded, I cannot conceal an impression which was forced upon me that it seemed to be assumed that a wounded man could find his own way back to the ambulances, wherever they might be placed. As a consequence, many men died from the neglect of comparatively slight wounds; even more, perhaps, than from more serious casualties, for a man so badly hit as to be unable to move at all generally found two or three comrades ready to carry him to the rear, where he always found proper bearers to convey him to the ambulance. But these were generally as carefully hidden and as far from the scene of the actual fighting as the corps commander and his chief of the staff.

When some poor wounded man was seen struggling painfully out of fire, he was allowed to do the best he could for himself without aid; and what

was worse, no one could point out to him, for it
had not been notified in general or regimental orders
the day before the fight, where the ambulance-
wagons would be placed.   Many a man gets a
wound that without surgical aid may prove mortal,
without remaining on the field, for it is astonishing
what superhuman exertions were induced amongst
the Russian wounded by the fear of being tortured
or bayoneted by the Turks.

It was cruelly hard on these poor fellows to have
to wander for miles to the rear in the hopeless search
for ambulance-wagons and medical care, which ought
to have been ready for them, if not in the front line,
certainly within sight of any man who fell.   I
believe that our army surgeons calculate on saving
ten per cent. of patients who have to undergo serious
operations in the field ; but I can state as a fact that
the Russian superior medical officers were well
content if they succeeded in saving one in a hundred.   There was always too much chloroform, or
too little, or some other trifling circumstance which
turned the balance against the unfortunate patients,
who died under the hands of their would-be saviours
with a promptitude that was appalling.

I saw on one occasion three cases of amputating

legs, in which a kindly "sister" stood by with a sponge supposed to be charged with chloroform, which she held to the man's nose. In each case she was surprised to see the poor fellows sit up and contemplate the doctors and herself, without any sign of anæsthesia supervening, the doctors having been too much occupied to see to charging the sponge, though they gave me to understand that the successful issue depended very much on chloroform being properly administered.

For a time after the third attack on Plevna, the Roumanians were even worse off than the Russians for surgical care. They had been hurried into war with very inadequate medical preparations, and suffered all the sad consequences. Indeed, at the very moment when some thousands of badly wounded men were thrown suddenly on their hands by the attack on Gravitza, there were no Roumanian ambulances actually at the front, and, as a consequence, all who could be got out from under the fire of the Turks were brought into the tents lying immediately under the great battery already mentioned by me as having been constructed by Colonel Exten, and under which Mr. Boyle of the *Standard* and myself had pitched our tents. I had, therefore,

an opportunity of watching the Russian surgeons
operating on their own men and on the Roumanians,
and was much struck by the difference in the behaviour of the men of the two nationalities. The
Russian was dogged, stolid, and silent, bearing
suffering almost with the stoical indifference of a
Red Indian ; while the slighter and more delicately-
organised Roumanians were querulous, soon lost
heart, and never could contemplate their wounds
without giving way to tears.

I must do the Russian surgeons the credit of
saying that, in the hopeless attempt to grapple with
the mass of suffering, they seemed to me to often
pass over their own men, and give the preference to
Roumanian soldiers. Whether it was the wailing of
the latter, or whether it was done out of pure
nobility of spirit, I leave those who are better acquainted with the Russian character to judge ; but
I am inclined to think that this preference was the
result of the utter contempt with which Russian
officers—and, indeed, the educated classes generally
—entertain for the lives of the individual soldier—
or of the classes beneath them. Though officers
are kind, and even generous to their men when in
the field, yet once hit, they fall out of notice, and

whether they live or die seems to be considered a matter of the smallest possible consequence. I saw myself, in many cases, when a surgeon had decided, after a very cursory examination, that a man was mortally wounded, the poor wretch was left to lie in agony and neglect till death put an end to his sufferings.

I had an account of the battle from Major Kavidka, who, as I have already mentioned, was the first to plant the Russian flag on the Gravitza height. He was shot through the upper part of the chest ; but he seemed to suffer much less from his wounds than from the fear that, being only an undistinguished member of the staff, he might not get the much-coveted decoration of the St. George's Cross.

"You will see, you will see," he said to me, speaking in French, with the excitement that the fever of his wound had brought on, "that the fellows at Radenice will get the Cross, and that I shall be passed over." Radenice, I need not say, was the position occupied by the headquarters during the struggle, a place fifteen miles to the rear as the crow flies.

On the evening of the 12th I started to carry my

despatches to Bucharest. I remained there till the
22nd, and returning then to the front, found nothing
whatever doing; so, being somewhat invalided, I
gave myself leave of absence. I returned by way of
Vienna, where I spent a few days, and then brought
up at home, where I remained till the 5th of
October. Returning to Bucharest, I reached that
city on the day the body of the Duke of Leuchtenberg passed through on its way to Russia for inter-
ment.

It was with great regret I heard of the death of
this promising young nephew of the Emperor. I
had seen him some two months before at Gorny
Studen, having, in fact, been obliged to clear out of
my quarters to make room for him. But there
was, perhaps, some consolation to his august rela-
tives in his having died a soldier's death; for I
believe it was a fact that he bore within him the
seeds of fatal pulmonary disease, which would soon
have ended his life much more painfully. Dying as
he did, his loss was really of great use to the Imperial cause, as it showed that the members of
the Romanoff family did not spare themselves in
the conflict with their hereditary enemy. This
event and the *émeutes* at Constantinople did good

service in Russia, for they served to distract public attention and quiet the impatience of the people in the unfortunate period between the non-successes I have just described and the final capture of Plevna.

Towards the close of November I once more arrived at the head-quarters at Bogot, where living in a little Kurd tent, in a courtyard by the side of the road running to Poradim, the Grand Duke Nicholas and his imposing staff were waiting day after day until Osman Pacha should feel justified in surrendering the position he had so long and so sternly held. The weather broke while I was there, and a pitiful time I had of it. There was no shelter from the bitter sleet and snow and from the deep mud, but some straw in a thin transparent little Wimbledon tent.

It was Sunday morning when I arrived at Bogot, and as in duty bound, my first act was to call and pay my respects to Colonel Hassenkamf. Passing the two sentries at the gate of the courtyard, I came first upon three Kurd tents put together. An organ was playing inside, and priests were chanting a Russian hymn. Outside the grounds the officers, cap in hand kneeling in the mud, were praying,

and farther back a fringe of soldiers in their
sheepskin coats, looking dirty and fierce, were re-
ligiously crossing themselves.   A little farther on
was Hassenkamf's tent, and from it he came out
to me with all that frankness of manner for which
the Russian Chief of Police is so justly celebrated.

"Ah! mon cher M. Stanley, c'est vous?"

"Yes, Colonel," I said, "I have heard that a letter
has been attributed to me by my patron of the
Golos, and as I cannot guess the purport of it,
or the consequences which appear to have resulted
from it, I have come to you to ask you what it is
all about."

He then went on to explain, saying:

"It appears you left Bucharest on the 22nd of
September, as General Skobeloff assured me that
he invited you to dinner, and that you dined with
him and General Ghourko, and several other officers
of the Guards, on that night, at a farewell dinner
which he offered to you previous to your leaving for
England.   Knowing this, we were much surprised
to find an erudite and most able letter dated from
Poradim on the 22nd of September, carefully sum-
ming up the faults which had been committed during
the campaign, giving to every one not only his fair

share of blame, but refusing merit to all, and not even sparing in its abuse the sacred person of his Majesty; also drawing invidious comparisons between the hereditary Grand Duke and the Grand Duke Nicholas. A letter, mon cher M. Stanley, which, with all the respect I feel for your talents, I don't think you were capable of writing; for it contained little matters which could only have been known to some one who had access to the staff and state papers."

"If you think that, my dear Colonel," said I, "why did you kick me out?"

"Because," said he, "when we saw this letter we telegraphed to the Minister of the Interior, and asked the editor of the *Golos* who had written it; and the reply sent, with the most charming promptitude, was, 'Our correspondent, Stanley.' We telegraphed back again to the Minister of the Interior: 'It cannot be, because Stanley is not here.'"

I did not hint to the gallant Colonel what a more extended acquaintance with correspondents will enable him probably to find out for himself, that presence in the flesh is not at all necessary to some of them to write graphically of places and events they have never seen.

He continued : " We then telegraphed, ' If it is Stanley who wrote that article, he need not come back to Bulgaria, for he is expelled.' "

" Well," said I, " Colonel, I did not not write that letter ; and the fact is, after your wonderful failure to make progress in September, having nothing good to write about, and being thoroughly tired and sick of the whole business, I wrote but one letter, and then went back to England ; but that letter was not to the *Golos*."

" Well," said he, " will you see the Grand Duke ? But what have you come out here now for ?"

I said, " I am here for the *Golos*, and also for one or two English papers.   Can I go down to see General Skobeloff."

That gallant officer was then at the front.

He replied : " The moment you assure me that you were not the author of that letter, of course your number and your position is restored to you."

The next morning I rode out to see General Skobeloff, and on my return, after trying to brush the mud off my boots and make myself as clean and respectable as I could, I presented myself before the little Kurd tent of his Imperial Highness the Grand Duke Nicholas.   Here I met Colonel

Hassenkamf again, and after some ten minutes in company with General Todleben, who was also waiting an audience, I was conducted into the Imperial presence.

The Grand Duke was sitting at a small table, with two candles burning before him, looking at the pictures in a number of the *Graphic*. Behind him, separated by a low screen, were two orderlies and a Russian general officer.

When I went in the Grand Duke dropped the paper, and clutching with both hands the lower part of the table, without waiting until I had had time to be presented—though, having seen him already at Tirnova, that ceremony was in some degree unnecessary—he called out, referring to the offensive letter which had appeared in the *Golos*, in English: " What *audace*, what *audace* is this ?"

I presumed to suggest the word "audacity" as the one he wanted to employ, and without appearing to notice the suggestion he repeated :

" What audacity is this ? It is like casting dirt upon my head."

" Monseigneur," I replied, feeling somewhat taken aback at the suddenness of the attack, " I have

already assured Colonel Hassenkamf that I did
not write that letter, and I can only repeat that
assurance.   As I had nothing good to say in
September, I went away in order that I might say
nothing."

"Le coquin," continued the Grand Duke, breaking off into French, in which he is clearly more at
home, though he speaks English very correctly,
"in that letter which you say you did not write, it
is pretended that I ordered up Monseigneur's army
from the Lom to my support at Plevna. Where
did you learn that?"

"Monseigneur," I replied, "I can only repeat
that I did not write that letter.

"Well, then," said he, "take my assurance that as
a man of honour you ought to punish those who
put your name to it."

"Well, I am going to St. Petersburg," I said,
"and I shall be happy to do everything I can to
put this matter straight, for I quite understand that
no one has the right to make use of my name in my
absence."

"Ah! you are going to St. Petersburg." Then
turning to Hassenkamf he said, "Draw me out a
letter to the Minister of the Interior, recommending

Stanley to his good graces." Then changing the conversation, he said : " I have just seen two very agreeable young countrymen of yours, Doctors Douglas and Vachell, with whom I was very much pleased ; but there was another of your compatriots who has been fighting against me, a Colonel. Do you know him ?"

I replied I did not know any of these gentlemen.

The Grand Duke went on then to say he had been much pleased with the way in which the two young English surgeons had stuck by each other while prisoners in his camp.

After a little more general conversation, during which he entirely recovered serenity of temper, he nodded and said " Au revoir," and as I left the tent called out in English : " Horrid weather, very horrid weather." As beyond all question it was.

I learnt after leaving the Grand Duke's presence that the name of the Colonel to whom he had referred was Coope, who ought to be thankful he got off as well as he did. I don't suppose he ever contemplated the possible consequences of such a procedure, but he was taken prisoner with a Turkish Gendarmerie commission in his pocket, and an ambulance *brassard* on his arm, and it was a question whether he might not be considered a spy.

I believe the Grand Duke asked Sir Henry Havelock to go and see if he knew him, and Sir Henry being obliged to say that he did not, it became a question at head-quarters how he was to be disposed of, and the Grand Duke, though by no means satisfied, sent him off as a prisoner of war to Russia, where I believe he was soon released at the intercession of Lord Augustus Loftus.

The *Golos* matter ended in this wise. I went to St. Petersburg, and a letter was sent to the Minister of the Interior, followed by repeated telegrams, so that I had not arrived at my hotel more than two hours before I was visited by Trepoff's chief man, who came to ask me, from the Minister of the Interior, what my views were as to the conduct of the *Golos* people.

I was very ill at the time, but I diplomatised as well as I could, and when he saw that I was too ill to leave my bed he left me. I then crawled out and taking a drosky drove over to the *Golos* office, where I had an amusing interview with the two chiefs. I dropped into the office like a bomb-shell, and on my charging them with forging my name to the offending article, they declared that they could produce the original letter.

I challenged them to do so, and then they said they were not sure whether it was written by me or by Mr. MacGahan of the *Daily News*, who was also a contributor to the *Golos*.

On my assuring them that the Grand Duke had stated that there were matters contained in the letter which could only have been known to himself and to the staff, they were obliged to give up this contention. They began then to think that the affair smacked somewhat of Siberia, and were, beyond all question, in a decided fright.

I then suggested that it would be much better for them, inasmuch as the letter had passed the censor, either to make a frank avowal of the matter and throw the whole responsibility on the censor; or to declare the real author's name. In any case I required a letter from them exonerating me from having written anything of the kind.

They then confided to me that the letter had been written by a member of the Imperial Staff, whose name even they mentioned, and it was then decided that they should go before the *Bureau de la Presse* and make a statement that I had nothing to do with writing the letter, and that the censor must take the responsibility of allowing it to be published.

On the following day I received a letter from another agent of M. Trepoff's, in which it was intimated that as I had not taken the Imperial view of the matter and lent myself to the prosecution of Messieurs the proprietors of the *Golos*, I had therewith my papers sent to me, and, ill as I was, I was obliged forthwith to leave St. Petersburg.

I have already mentioned Monsieur de Nelidow, the accredited political agent and adviser to the Grand Duke, and as I at many and different times had opportunities of conversing with him and learning his views, it may be well if I give a short sketch of a conversation which I had the honour of holding with him at Bagot towards the close of November, and which was introduced by a question on my part as to the meaning of the Emperor again summoning to his councils the dreaded and wily Ignatieff. He replied :

" General Ignatieff was never, either through the intrigues of his enemies or the disfavour of the Emperor, dismissed the Imperial head-quarters, as is generally asserted ; the facts are that the Emperor

overheard the General say on one occasion when at
the Imperial breakfast-table, that he was suffering
greatly from dysentery and rheumatism. With
that loving thoughtfulness inherent in his character,
the Emperor turned to the General and said,
' Prenez congé ; allez dans vos terres.' The General
accepted, and went first to his government at Kieff,
and afterwards to see his father, the President of the
Council of Ministers, at St. Petersburg. He continued in the high favour of the Empress, and was
the instrument chosen to signify to the venerable
General Todleben the opinion of his Majesty that
the talents of that eminent soldier were required
to aid in overcoming the difficulties at Plevna."

Fully satisfied with the explanation, though still
retaining in my own mind, from something I had
heard elsewhere, the idea that General Ignatieff had
been temporarily cashiered by the influence of the
Grand Duke Nicholas, and on the assumption that
he had misled the Russian military authorities as to
the actual strength and capability of Turkey for
defence, I turned the attention of his Excellency
to the great distrust which prevailed in England
regarding the intentions of Russia when Turkey
should be compelled to sue for peace.

He began by reminding me (as did all the Russian politicians, it was in fact the regular stock joke) of the solemn assurance given by the Emperor to Lord Augustus Loftus at Livadia, and of the distinct pledges given by his Majesty since, that the sole object of the war was to ensure the proper treatment of the Christians. He then dwelt upon the close affinity and fellow-feeling existing between the Christians of Bulgaria and of parts of Asiatic Turkey and the lower classes of the Russian people, insisting that it was these classes and not the so-called war-party at St. Petersburg who had urged on the war, and were really responsible for it. He said that the Emperor would be in nowise tempted by the success that might attend his arms to form notions of aggrandisement, but that his promise not to make acquisitions of territory applied only to Europe.

I here said that having carefully read the formal despatch of Prince Gortschakoff, endorsing the promises at Livadia made to the English ambassador, as well as the reply of Lord Derby to the same, it appeared to me that our foreign minister interpreted the Czar's words to mean an absolute promise that no annexation of any kind or anywhere would be attempted by Russia.

" Not so," replied Monsieur de Nelidow, " your ambassador requested assurances at Livadia as to the general purport of the war, which was answered by the sentence ' Liberation of the Christians from the Mussulman yoke.' He further asked what destiny was reserved for the liberated provinces, and was answered by the word ' autonomy.' If your ambassador wanted further assurances, he should have asked for them ; but he appeared quite contented with the pledge given by the Emperor not to extend his dominions in Europe beyond their limits in 1856. The English," he went on to say (evidently looking on Asia as a sort of no-man's land) " held on to all they acquired in India, whether gained by bargaining or by arms." And so the Czar ; having given no pledge as to Armenia, Russia would be justified, in his opinion, in holding on to all she should acquire by conquest in Asia. Neither could he see why England should object.

I intimated that a reasonable fear existed in England that Russia would in such an event seek to improve her success in Armenia by extending her

sway in the direction of the Levant, and endeavour
to become a Mediterranean power by forcing herself
towards Smyrna. Monsieur de Nelidow admitted
that the turning or flanking of the Dardanelles by
way of Smyrna, was a question of great nicety for
the politicians of the future—say some quarter of a
century hence—but that as Russia had at present
no wish to see the whole western world in
arms against her, such fears were for the moment
idle.

Touching on the cession of the Turkish fleet, my
interlocutor remarked that while Russia might insist
on the Sultan getting rid of a great portion of his
fleet, as the Ottoman ruler would no longer require
it, there was no idea of a compulsory cession to
Russia; in fact, Russia had no need of so great a
fleet as the cession of the Turkish, in addition to
her own, would give her. My mind involuntarily
ran towards " sour grapes " as I bowed myself
out.

CHAPTER X.

STANDING one day in October in the main street of
Bucharest in conversation with a Russian general
officer, at the time when an infantry three-battalion
regiment and a couple of batteries of the Imperial
Guard were defiling before General Ghourko, who,
with his staff, was posted opposite the National
Theatre, the General said to me : " Once let those
fellows reach Plevna and get across the Sophia
road, and you may reckon the campaign as good as
ended."

Though matters were not at that time looking so
badly for the Turks, I could not help admitting

that there was a great deal of likelihood in this proposition. I ventured to suggest, however, that as Osman Pacha had so far shown himself singularly able and energetic, there was no reason to suppose that he would allow himself to be quite shut in, unless he was well assured that he was doing the best for his cause by keeping so large a force of Russians and Roumanians round his beleaguered stronghold, and that he might rely on sufficient outside assistance to break through when the right time arrived.

" Nous verrons ce que nous verrons," said the General ; and the world did see a grand defence, which will ever occupy a high position in military annals.

Honourable as was the reputation achieved by Osman Pacha, it yet disappointed those who, from his able advance on, and defence of Plevna, gave him credit for the highest qualities of generalship. No one doubts now that he ought to have evacuated Plevna when the Imperial Guard began to arrive, and to have fallen back along the Sophia road, choosing in the Balkans a position which a few days would have made equally impregnable to direct attack, while it would have so lengthened the line of Russian communications, that the first downpour of rain would have made it impossible to feed any considerable body of troops. What did happen is now matter of history.

The Imperial Guard—the very pick and flower of the Russian army—duly arrived. One may mention, however, *en passant*, that though the battalions were up to their full strength of 1000 each, it was obvious that, to attain this result, a number of small men had been taken into the ranks who would have found no place there in time of peace. They were promptly placed, *à cheval*, across the only practicable line of retreat for the now beleaguered Turks; and then ensued the wearisome process of effecting by starvation what experience had shown could not be done by direct assault.

For long weeks, through a splendid season of Indian summer, which seemed almost providentially in favour of the Russians—for if a rainy season had set in as early as it often does in Bulgaria, most of the besiegers must have fallen back on the Danube to avoid starvation—the iron circle round Plevna was strengthened and drawn closer and closer, every day diminishing the chance of a successful sortie.

The allies always professed to be well acquainted

15

with the progress of affairs in Plevna ; and by the
middle of November it was asserted that provisions
had already become so scarce, that the men were on
quarter-rations, so that the end must be near.   Towards the end of the month capitulation was thought
to be only a question of hours ; and the garrison
were said to be in such a melancholy condition, that
the Grand Duke Nicholas telegraphed in hot haste
to the Russian Intendance to forward instantly to
head-quarters an ample supply of biscuits, to feed the
mass of starving prisoners that were sure to be soon
in his hands.   This thoughtful and humane proceeding was followed a very few days later by Prince
Charles of Roumania, who made similar provision
for the proportion of prisoners that would fall to
his charge.

Meantime the long season of fine weather came to
an end ; driving rain-storms, heavy fogs, and a very
low temperature caused great suffering amongst the
besiegers.   Every day saw long trains of sick
jolting painfully through the heavy roads, in spring-
less country wagons, to the already over-crowded
hospitals of Turnu-Magurelli, frost-bite in many
cases complicating the diseases from which they
were suffering.   Day after day passed away, but

there was no sign of sortie, or of what the besiegers —while, to do them justice, omitting no precautions against a sortie—believed would really terminate this long episode in the war—namely, a capitulation, without any active attempt to break through the lines of investment.

December came; and before a week had elapsed, unmistakable signs appeared of one of those heavy snow-falls which in the country north of the Balkans are often of almost incredible severity. Night and day unremitting watch was kept on the grim outline of Turkish redoubts and trenches, from which for days past no reply had now been made to the intermittent fire from the Russian and Roumanian siege-guns.

Inside Plevna, matters, though never so bad as they had been represented by the allies, had, by the 8th of December, come to a crisis. Osman Pacha and his troops had begun to be somewhat discouraged when the news reached them of the capture of Kars; but the "Ghazi" himself reckoned confidently on receiving aid from outside up to the 2nd of December. Then came undoubted intelligence of the operations of the Russian troops in the neighbourhood of Orkhanie; and the unwelcome

conviction was forced upon him that there was no
hope of retreat in the direction of Sophia.   The only
chance left to him—and this he was soldier enough
to be perfectly aware was a very slender chance
indeed—was to cut his way out to the north-west,
and make for Widdin.   He was unaware that
Rahova had fallen into the hands of the Roumanians, and that instead of being strengthened
by effecting a junction, as he anticipated, with
the garrison of that place, it was held by enemies,
who, to the extent of their means, would inevitably
fall upon the flank of his retreating forces, if ever
they got so far.

He determined to try his desperate venture on
the night of the 9th-10th of December.   His sick
and wounded were left behind, all useless arms and
cannon were stored in the town, and with his fighting force, which numbered some sixty tabors, or
40,000 men, each supplied with 150 rounds of ammunition and six days' rations of biscuits, he concentrated during the night of the 9th on the Vid,
where, with immense labour and very inadequate
materials—for a few planks and native wagons were
all the pontooning appliances at his disposal—two
bridges were thrown over the river.

It was pretended that the Russians were cognisant of all that was going on, and that they offered no opposition, but calmly awaited the attack, in the full confidence of being able to drive the Turks back. The facts are, however, that the allies expected that a sortie might take place two nights before, and then much more decided preparations were made for repelling it, from the moment any movement became developed.

Day and night on the 7th of December, the trenches of the besiegers had been kept filled with troops; posts were doubled, and in some cases trebled. Divisional generals and commanders of regiments were specially warned from head-quarters that they would be held responsible for any failure to instantly detect a movement amongst the enemy.

Saturday, the 8th of December, was passed in this state of extreme tension, which was manifested by somewhat more than usual activity on the part of the batteries, to which the Turks, as usual, made no reply. Sunday opened in much the same fashion, and when, soon after noon, a snow-storm began, there was a general sense of relief, arising from an impression that the expected sortie was a false alarm.

During the afternoon, the Russian soldiers were especially gleeful, singing songs and comparing notes about home; which the falling snow and rapidly whitening ground perhaps helped to bring more prominently to their recollection. In Plevna, the only special sign of activity was the slender columns of light blue smoke which, ascending perhaps more thickly than usual, were yet rather more suggestive of cooking rations and people making themselves comfortable, than of the commencement of a desperate sortie. If statements in certain Russophile journals in London are to be believed, the Russians were so well served by their spies, that on the Sunday they were informed that Osman's troops were being supplied with rations, cartridges, and even oil, to lubricate their rifles, and that the movement had hardly commenced, before they knew of the concentration on the Vid.

The real facts of the case are as follows. An alarm of an intended sortie had spread amongst the allies on the 6th of December, and as it was perfectly clear that the movement could only take place to the westward, both Russians and Roumanians had concentrated troops in positions to move rapidly on the threatened points, relying on the field-telegraph which connected the head-quarters with the camp of each general of division, for issuing the necessary orders when the Turkish movement was actually developed.

The first really authentic information obtained by the Russians, came to Skobeloff about four a.m. on Monday, when a skulking deserter was brought into his head-quarters with the news of the Turks having deserted the Krishine redoubt, and all their lines in front of that gallant General's position. He at once satisfied himself that the news was true, and then taking possession of the redoubts and lines, and proceeding actively to put them in a state of defence, he at once wired the news to head-quarters. It was not, however, till the thunder of artillery, followed almost immediately by the crashing, continuous roll of musketry from the Vid, just as day broke, that it became known that the sortie had actually begun. Then it was soon seen that all the Turkish positions, from Gravitza to the Green Hill, were deserted, and that the Turks, who had so long gallantly held them, were over the river, advancing over the wide plain against the positions held by the grenadiers of the Imperial Guard, extending north from the Sophia road to opposite Opanes, where they effected a junction with the Roumanian lines. The first intimation that the grenadiers had of the sortie, was seeing a line of bullock-wagons advancing directly upon them, with a deployed line of Turks in rear, as if availing themselves of the wagons as a shelter to get to close quarters with their foe.

Without the loss of a moment, the Russian guns belched out a storm of shell and shrapnel, while the infantry stood to their arms, and speedily poured in a continuous shower of bullets from their Berdan breechloaders.

A few minutes sufficed to destroy the symmetry of the line of wagons. Many of the cattle dropped dead or wounded; others started off in all directions, in a fright at the bursting shells; while not a few turned back in the direction they had come. Disengaging themselves from this rout of wagons and bullocks, the Turks, with their war-cry of " Allah-il-allah," charged straight at the intrenchments held by the Siberian grenadiers. Though falling fast under the *feu-d'enfer* of the Berdan, they swept in with a rush, bayoneting nearly the whole regiment, and killing all the artillerymen, most of whom died at their guns.

Scarcely, however, had this brilliant feat of arms

been performed, and before they had time to advance
to the attack of the double line of intrenchments
which they would still have had to carry before they
were out of the toils, when a brigade of Russian
grenadiers came to the rescue. After a few volleys,
the grenadiers charged at the captured battery and
trenches, and a bayonet-fight of rare duration ensued. Two or three times the battery was taken
and retaken at the point of the bayonet, the Turks
clinging to it with desperate tenacity. They were,
however, heavily outnumbered.

Russian reinforcements kept pouring in, and soon
so murderous a fire was developed, that the gallant
Turks were driven out of the trenches; all who held
to the battery were killed, mostly by the bayonet,
and they were speedily forced to retreat. Staying
for a short time behind the line of wagons, which
afforded some shelter, they essayed to return the
fire; but still losing many men from the continuous
hail of Russian bullets, the survivors again retreated
towards the river, which runs between banks sufficiently high to afford them the shelter they so
much needed.

This repulse of Osman's advanced guard virtually
decided the fate of the sortie. The Plevna side of

the plain is bounded by steep cliffs overhanging the river, and one deep gorge leading to the town of Plevna, and from these, for a distance of two miles on either side, there came the unceasing flash and roar of artillery, while in the narrow valley below the main body of the Turks were assailed on either side by the rifle-fire of constantly increasing masses of the allies.

All retreat was cut off by their redoubts and trenches having been occupied the moment they were known to be deserted ; while a column of Roumanians had penetrated right into Plevna itself, and occupied the road by which the sortie had been made.

By half-past eight in the morning, the fate of the attempt was decided ; but, for four hours longer, the Turks, from the shelter of the river-banks, continued the battle. Then, as if by mutual consent, the storm of shells and the hail of bullets began to abate, and finally stopped altogether, as if both sides had exhausted their ammunition.

Very soon after, a white flag was seen waving from the road on the Plevna side of the bridge, and the joyful tidings spread like lightning amongst the Russians that the army of Osman Pacha was about to surrender. Loud shouts, of which there was no mistaking the signification, went up from the serried Muscovite ranks, and the men shook hands with each other at the thoughts of their dreary vigils round Plevna being at an end.

Very soon a mounted Turkish officer rode over the bridge bearing the flag of truce, and communicated with the General commanding the grenadiers who were posted opposite the bridge. He soon returned, however, in search of an officer of superior rank, qualified to treat for a capitulation.

Many Russian officers, including General Skobeloff, who had brought up the best part of his command as reinforcement, rode towards the bridge. Beyond were masses of Turkish infantry, rifle in hand, lining the road and on the face of the cliff above; and if they had felt inclined to be bellicose, the situation of these adventurous few would have been anything but enviable.

Skobeloff and two of his staff waved white handkerchiefs, and must have experienced no inconsiderable relief on seeing that their peaceful overtures were accepted by similar signs. Very soon, two Turkish orderlies, each carrying a white flag, came along the road, crossed the bridge, and approached

the group of Russian officers. There was a brief
colloquy between them and an interpreter attached
to Skobeloff's staff, when the two horsemen turned
their horses and cantered back, and the interpreter
announced that Osman was wounded, and was himself coming out.

Very shortly, two mounted men again made
their appearance, but this time with a single flag of
truce borne by one of them—a soldier, wearing the
universal fez, a shabby brown cloak, and sandals of
raw hide on his feet. The other horseman had on a
new fez, the blue cloth cloak of an officer, and wore
new gloves; he was newly shaven and washed, and
had light blue eyes, a long fair moustache, and a
bright, intelligent face that prepossessed one directly
in his favour. It was Tefik Bey, the chief of Osman's
staff, to whom, of course, much of the credit of the
splendid defence of Plevna was fairly due. Speaking French, but with much hesitation, as if he had
to think for each word before he uttered it, he acknowledged the frank, soldierly greetings of the
Russian officers, stated who he was, and announced,
what had not been before made quite clear, that
Osman Pacha was shot in the leg, and was then in a
small house just over the bridge, which he pointed out.

Then there ensued a somewhat long and embarrassing pause, which was not ended by an attempt on the part of some of the group to induce Tefik Bey to enter into conversation. General Strukoff of the Emperor's staff soon came up, and having power to treat, entered into conversation with Tefik Bey on the subject of capitulation ; and the result was that Tefik, who did not appear to be vested with equivalent powers, quickly turned his horse's head and galloped back to the house he had indicated. Meantime the *gros* of the Russian infantry had moved towards the bridge, and the rival lines of troops stood watching each other at not more than quarter of a mile's distance. Happily neither side seemed inclined to renew the strife, or the situation of the group at the bridge would have been critical in the extreme. Soon after, some of the Turkish infantry, rifle in hand or hanging by the sling from their shoulders, strolled over the bridge, came up to the group of officers and walked round surveying them with evident curiosity ; while their comrades by thousands on the cliffs close by, stared coolly and composedly in the same direction.

The only sign of capitulation so far was the occupation by the Russians of a redoubt up on high ground

which the enemy had taken in their advance, the
Turks leaving their hardly-won prize on one side as
the victorious Muscovites marched in on the other.
Generals Ganetsky and Strukoff next moved towards
the bridge to the house where Osman Pacha was
lying wounded, to have an interview with him. The
group of officers followed them at some little distance,
but the pressure was very great, and the road was
blocked with dead and dying men, oxen, horses, and
with shattered wagons, through which it was difficult
to find a path.

A few minutes sufficed to arrange matters with
Osman Pacha, for the capitulation was unconditional.
His army was in an irretrievable fix, jammed together
in the narrow valley of the Vid, while his enemies,
who were every moment increasing in numbers by the
arrival of reinforcements, occupied the heights on
either side, and hopelessly stopped the outlet of
the gorge. Resistance would have been simple madness, for the Turks were even more effectually
inclosed than were the French at Sedan.

Osman was suffering from his wound, and he was
therefore soon after two p.m. assisted to a carriage
and taken back to Plevna for medical treatment.
The news of the surrender was soon spread amongst

the Turks, and when ordered by their officers to lay down their arms, they obeyed the injunction to the letter by pitching their splendid rifles into the mud, where thousands of them were trampled into the deep mire and irretrievably ruined.

The Grand Duke Nicholas and his staff soon after arrived, and passed in review the troops, specially congratulating the grenadiers, who had stopped Osman's advance. On his way into Plevna, the Grand Duke encountered the captured Turkish General. Hearing that the Commander-in-Chief was following him, Osman Pacha ordered the carriage to turn, and escorted by a Cossack guard of fifty men, and surrounded by a group of his own officers, all riding Turkish ponies, went to meet the victor. The Grand Duke rode straight to the carriage door, and after gazing for a second or so at the gallant Turk, stretched out his hand with a soldierlike frankness that evidently affected the prisoner, and grasping that of Osman, which he shook cordially, complimented him on his defence of Plevna as one of the greatest military feats in history. Osman smiled painfully, and in spite of his wound struggled to his feet, uttered a few words of acknowledgment, amid hearty and unanimous "bravos"

of the Russian staff, the group of Russian officers
saluting him as respectfully ; but he was obliged,
by his wound, to resume his seat directly.   Prince
Charles of Roumania came up before the incident
had terminated, and complimented Osman in almost
the same words as the Grand Duke.   Again the
wounded man struggled to his feet, merely, however,
to bow with constrained courtesy, and an expression
of face that typified the very different feelings enter-
tained by the Turks for the Roumanians, whom they
regarded as rebellious subjects of their own, and for
their old and avowed Muscovite enemies.   During
this incident a good opportunity was afforded of
seeing what manner of man it was that had for
months arrested the Russian invasion in Europe.
Osman Pacha is a large, powerful man, so stoutly
built as to make him appear scarcely up to the
middle height.   His face is of a type common
amongst the Osmanli Turks—large and broad, with
strongly-marked features, high Roman nose, deep
black eyes, and thick black beard, cut close.   Intelligence and indomitable determination are impressed
on every lineament ; but the long period of anxiety
through which he had passed in conducting so grand
a defence, with very little assistance from his staff,

had graven deep lines, and given a careworn expression to a face which some of his own officers said looked ten years older than when he marched from Widdin.

The Turkish prisoners were mustered as soon as possible after laying down their arms, and bivouacked on the plains beyond the Vid, guarded by Russian and Roumanian troops. On the following day a *Te Deum* was celebrated in presence of the Emperor, the Grand Duke, Prince Charles, and their respective suites, in one of the redoubts, and prayers were offered up for those who had fallen. After this ceremony, the Emperor breakfasted in a Bulgarian house, when Osman Pacha was sent for. The Turkish General was received with the highest respect, the whole of the officers present rising and saluting, as he was carried in by two Turkish officers. He was complimented by the Emperor as highly as he had been on the previous day by the Grand Duke, and the Czar, handing him his scimetar, told him to wear it while he remained a prisoner in Russia. When the wounded hero was removed, there was a general cry of " Bravo !" from the Russian officers, who saluted again as he was carried to his carriage.

Osman was soon after moved by easy stages to Bucharest, and thence, after remaining a few days, to Russia by railway. His unfortunate troops were marched to the Danube, and thence into Roumania. The Russian Intendance, never very remarkable for success in their functions, seem to have pretty nearly ignored the requirements of these unfortunates, who were in a state of semi-starvation when they encountered a fearful snow-storm, and being wholly without shelter, and very scantily clad, they perished by hundreds on the roads, and thousands of the survivors were affected by frost-bite before they reached Bucharest.

Outside of Plevna, though pitiful scenes of human suffering were rife, one only encountered what may fairly be described as the heroic side of warfare; but inside there was a woeful change of scene.

Those who first penetrated into Plevna after the capitulation saw a panorama of horrors, of which the most graphic pen would fail to convey an adequate idea. Men dying of wounds and disease were lying helpless and broadcast in every street, while others, who with moderate care might have been easily cured, were beyond help, more from absolute starvation than from hurts or from ailments.

Houses were crowded with dead in every stage of corruption ; no burials apparently having taken place long previous to the sortie. Thousands of the sick and wounded, who were nominally in hospital, had really been nearly uncared for from the moment that they succumbed, for up to the time of the complete investment the Turks had periodically sent the wounded on by convoy to Sophia, there being only a small and very inefficient ambulance corps in Plevna itself. When preparations for the sortie began, the ambulance people simply gave over all attention to their unhappy charges, joined the troops in the hope of breaking through the Rusian lines, and were made prisoners.

All Sunday and Monday passed, and the unfortunates remained unfed and untended. On Tuesday the Russians and Roumanians took possession of the town, and rejoiced exceedingly, the Emperor and his staff entering and joining in the celebration of the victory. The feeble cries and entreaties of the mass of suffering wretches who were lying everywhere, some in hospitals, but more in the open streets, were wholly unheeded, and they perished by hundreds.

On the third day the victors began leisurely to

16—2

separate the living from the dead, and tardily to extend a little care to the former. More than one-third were found to have perished when the first rough separation was made, and the proportion went on increasing hourly by the deaths of those to whom help had come too late. The state of the poor wretches who lay amid slush and snow in the open air was horrible enough; but it was infinitely preferable to that of those who still survived in the ghastly hospitals, where living and dead were shut up together in an atmosphere so reeking with putrid odours from undressed wounds and the inevitable filth of total neglect, that strong men staggered back faint and sick on attempting to enter. It required no small determination to drag the dead from these horrible apartments, to throw wide open doors and windows, and remove the horrible accumulations which were poisoning the air.

All that the unhappy survivors could obtain to give them a chance of life was a morsel of hard black bread and a little water, and even this was so sparingly served out that some of the poor wretches, who had yet a little strength left in their emaciated frames, fought and wrangled for the possession of a

stray bit, while others dropped dead in the attempt
to eat, furnishing occasion for another pitiful
scramble amongst the survivors.

A few ox-carts and a fatigue-party of soldiers
were set to work to bury the bodies; but they
failed to dispose of the corpses as rapidly as the
hospitals supplied them with fresh freight, and then
a number of Bulgarian peasants were pressed into
the horrible service. These brutes seemed to take a
pleasure in treating the bodies of the dead Turks
with the greatest possible amount of indignity.
Taking the body by the legs, they dragged it down-
stairs, bumping the head on every step, through the
mire of the street, to pitch it *pêle-mêle* into the ox-
wagon. Many cases occurred in which men still
living were dragged in this way to the wagon and
pitched in, the fact of life not being extinct being
observed and commented on.

When filled with corpses the wagons started
through the streets, now teeming again with the
inhabitants and soldiers, bodies occasionally dropping
out and being tossed in again and stamped down to
prevent a similar accident. The utter want of
system which characterised all the Russian arrangements allowed these scenes to go on for weeks after

the fall of Plevna. That and the miserable fate of the prisoners, who were bivouacked in a starving condition for days on the plain west of the Vid, and then marched off, without food, to perish in the snow, will for ever remain a monument of eternal disgrace to the Russian name.

THE END.

BILLING AND SONS, PRINTERS, GUILDFORD, SURREY.

S. & II.

www.ingramcontent.com/pod-product-compliance
Lightning Source LLC
Chambersburg PA
CBHW020057030726
47498CB00006B/1827